Flippin' In

&

Then and Now

by Anne Chislett

Playwrights Canada Press
Toronto Canada

Flippin' In © Copyright 1999 Anne Chislett
Then and Now © Copyright 1999 Anne Chislett

Playwrights Canada Press
54 Wolseley Street, 2nd Floor
Toronto, Ontario CANADA M5T 1A5
(416) 703-0201   fax (416) 703-0059
cdplays@interlog.com   http://www.puc.ca

Playwrights Canada Press acknowledges the support of The Canada Council for the Arts for our publishing programme and the Ontario Arts Council.

Cover design by Jodi Armstrong.

Canadian Cataloguing in Publication Data

Chislett, Anne
  Flippin' in, and, Then & now

Plays.
ISBN 0-88754-574-2

1. Children's plays, Canadian (English) – 20th century.* I. Title.
II. Title: Then and now. III. Title: Then and now.

PS8555.H57F56 1999   jC812'.54   C99-932003-3
PR9199.3.C4945F56 1999

Printed and bound by Hignell Printing
at Winnipeg, Manitoba, Canada.

Anne Chislett's plays have been produced across Canada and in the United States and Japan. *Quiet in the Land* won the Governor General's Award for Drama and the Chalmers Canadian Play award. *Flippin' In* also won the Chalmers Canadian Play Award in the Theatre For Young Audiences division. Other plays include *The Tomorrow Box*, *Yankee Notions* and *Another Season's Promise* (written with Keith Roulston.) Anne is currently Artistic Director of The Blyth Festival.

Flippin'

In

Flippin' In was commissioned by Young People's Theatre, Toronto, and first produced in 1996.

Cast:

JOE	Bruce Beaton
SUSAN	Christine Brubacker
LYNN	Rachel Lai
ELAINE	Monique Marcker
MARIA	Beatriz Pizano

Directed by Sally Han
Set and Costumes by Bill Ramussen

Musical Directors	Daryl Purdy and Shawn Bowring
Choreographer	Lisa Prebianca
Stage Manager	Michael Wallace

Flippin' In won the 1996 Chalmer's Canadian Play for Young Audiences' Award. It was subsequently produced by Geordie Productions, Ground Zero and Green Thumb.

The author wishes to acknowledge the invaluable assistance of Ester Reiter's book, *Making Fast Food*, published by McGill University Press.

Characters

SUSAN   17

LYNN   17

JOE   20-25

ELAINE   25-40

MARIA   25-50

Set

Props and set pieces should be consisently stylized to be light-weight and bright. There are lots of props, but think non-realistic minimalism.

MCJOBS

A gym, preset with two gear bags.

MARIA, an immigrant whom we might take for a school cleaner, wheels on the scoreboard. We read Markdale S.S. We read the score of the class teams. Blues: 31. Greens: 28. There should also be a calendar or device that can indicate weeks passing.

Sound. A referee's whistle; shouts of "Go!" "Let's Go! Go, go, go!" from classmates in the stands.

Two sixteen-year-old girls run on. Both wear T-shirts, one with a wildlife concern logo, the other a designer name. SUSAN, the girl who likes animals, has a green ribbon around her arm to denote her team. Lynn has a blue ribbon tied in a neat bow. Both are excited and tense in the last few seconds of the game. They react to invisible other players. Then SUSAN seizes the ball and makes a forceful dash for the basket. LYNN hesitates for a split second before leaping to block her. SUSAN shoots and scores.

MARIA changes the score. Blues: 31. Greens: 30. SUSAN regains the ball, ducks around LYNN, and sinks what would be the winning basket but—

Sound. The school bell and the P.E. Instructor's whistle cut short the game. Cheers and Boos.

LYNN   That's not fair. Your basket should have counted.

Girls pull off their ribbons and pick up their bags. LYNN's is trendier and more expensive than SUSAN's.

SUSAN   *(shrugging)* There's always next time.

> *SUSAN sets off outside with a purpose. LYNN seems to need to connect with her.*

LYNN   Susan... wanta come for a coke or something?

SUSAN   *(shaking her head)* I have to go to work.

LYNN   Oh, you're lucky.

SUSAN   See ya.

LYNN   *(refusing the dismissal)* I've been trying for a job for ages.

> *And this is surprise enough to make SUSAN pause.*

SUSAN   You?

LYNN   I've applied at the library, the newspaper, the copy shop...

SUSAN   *(with an edge)* Doesn't your father need another receptionist?

LYNN   You know he's cutting back.

SUSAN   *(knowing this all too well)* Yeah. *(with attitude)* Excuse me.

LYNN   I'm sorry Dad had to lay your mother off, Susan, but it was company policy... you know, orders from head office.

SUSAN   Yeah.

LYNN   Look, it wasn't his fault. *(pause)* And it's not mine either.

*JOE enters and leans on an imaginary corner.
He's a rock and rolling tough guy, ring in nose,
pins in ears, studs on jacket. He whistles after
the girls. LYNN glances over.*

SUSAN Hi, Joe.

LYNN *(incredulous)* Is he a friend of yours?

SUSAN *(shrugging)* Sort of. But what do you need to
work for?

LYNN For money of my own. I've a right, don't I?

SUSAN *(a concession)* I guess.

LYNN I cannot believe the way you suddenly treat me
like I'm a snob or something. *(starting off)* It's
just not fair.

SUSAN *(after her)* Lynn, ...well, actually, my boss might
be looking for someone.

*ELAINE, an attractive business woman in her
thirties, enters.*

ELAINE As long as you have a positive attitude, a
friendly personality, and you're willing to work
hard, there's a place for you in the Service
Industry.

*MARIA wheels the scoreboard around to display
a billboard of a giant hamburger and a smiling
worker.*

ALL McJobs!

KWIKBITEY: WORLD
A fast food Franchise

*JOE removes his tough guy accessories until he
looks clean cut. Then he and SUSAN and
MARIA pull typical fast food uniforms from
SUSAN's bag, and put them on over their clothes
as ELAINE begins patter #1. JOE, MARIA, and
SUSAN join in as they climb into the uniforms.*

Welcome to KwikWorld
The world of KwikHappy,
Where food is KwikCheap
And service is real Snappy.

From Vancouver Island to Bonavista Bay
From Moscow to Paris, from Lima, to L.A.
It's bread, meat and potatoes
And "Have a nice Day."

*During the following scene, MARIA wheels in
the needed set pieces and sets up props.*

ELAINE Lynn, tell me why you want to be part of Kwik-
Bitey's' family?

LYNN Well... I come here after school and movies and
that... and I think it would be great... *(smiling)*
because it's a great place.

JOE *(to SUSAN, incredulous)* She a friend of yours?

SUSAN *(shrugging)* Sort of.

ELAINE You know, you have a lovely smile.

**JOE &
SUSAN** She's hired.

ALL   We know no regional disparities,
We discount different views
What we sell is similarities
And happy KwikSnappy crews.

> *On the above line, ELAINE adds an Employee of the Month poster to the billboard.*

We are bigger than most nations
And a heck of a lot more fun
So take your places at the stations
And be part of Number One

ELAINE   We give you— *(presenting LYNN with a uniform from her own bag)* free uniforms!

LYNN   *(dismayed)* Polyester!

JOE   With no pockets.

ELAINE   And a free training video.

> *LYNN struggles into her uniform as the others act out the film. SUSAN could wear a mask as the actress, and JOE a customer's mask. The movements could be somewhat stylised.*

SUSAN   KwikWorld feature presentation! Starring...

JOE   *(donning a mask and bowing)* The happy KwikGuest...

SUSAN   That's customer in English.

ELAINE   It's up to Kwik-Bitey's team to make sure the guest has a positive mental image of our food.

> *All the dialogue with the exception of ELAINE's cheerleading, is rhythmic patter.*

JOE   Our KwikGuest's experience/ begins out of doors/ He sees no litter on the walkways/—

ELAINE drops a candy wrapper, and cheerleads as in the basketball game. MARIA scurries to pick it up.

ELAINE Let's go, gang.

JOE He'll see sparkling clean floors. /

ELAINE Go, go, go!

MARIA scurries to wipe the floor.

JOE Our KwikGuest enters at four forty-three. /

ELAINE From this point on, we take note of the timer. /

SUSAN The On-Counter KwikHostess—

ELAINE *(reprimanding her)* The nice smiling KwikHostess. / Read the tray liner / where it says—

LYNN *(searching)* Oh... *(reading)* oh—smiles are free! /

SUSAN *(donning a smiling mask)* Welcome to our restaurant. / May I take your order, please? /

JOE *(hamming it up)* I'll have a chocolate shake / and the big one with cheese. /

SUSAN A whopping big KwikKing, sir? /

JOE Yeah, that should suffice. /

ELAINE *(prompting)* And?

SUSAN And will you have some fries, sir? /

JOE Yeah, fries might be kinda nice. /

ELAINE *(to LYNN)* The profit-making order / includes French fries and a drink. / If KwikGuest omits an item / we need to make him think.

LYNN   Oh.

SUSAN   *(entering the order on the cash register)* Two dollars, fifty cents, sir./ Now, is that to go or stay?/ Depending on his answer/ grab a bag or grab a tray.

ELAINE   Cut to!

> *JOE takes off his mask and runs or jumps to the area we establish as the kitchen. MARIA takes a place along the grill.*

JOE   Meanwhile, back in the KwikKitchen, the computerised Kwik cash register has relayed the order to the cooking crew. In English, that's "grill toads."

ELAINE   Fries.

> *JOE and MARIA have a mime/dance/patter number which establishes the symbolic props and kitchen layout. The kitchen has a different rhythm.*

MARIA   *(speaking with an accent)* Thank you.

JOE   They came out of the freezer this morning/ they're in baskets all ready to go./ Pre-cut, measured, and coated with sugar/ to give them that yummy brown glow.

> *JOE lowers a basket and pushes a button.*

ELAINE   Cheeseburger.

> *MARIA places a burger on the grill.*

JOE   So you put down the heel/ and slap on the cheese/ then dab on the mustard/ give the ketchup a squeeze. *(squeezing twice)*

ELAINE *(correcting him)* One squeeze, and in a spiral
motion starting from the outside edge.

JOE Then you pick up the pickle/ and spoon on the
onion...

ELAINE Hold the pickle! Joe, can't you even get it right
in the video?

SUSAN The onion goes on first.

ELAINE Rewind.

*In fast backward motion JOE takes off the pickle
and scoops up the onion.*

Play.

JOE puts on the onion, then the pickle.

ELAINE People can taste the difference.

Sound. Buzzers and beeps.

JOE That sound tells you the fries are ready/ this
one signals the burger is done./ You put it
together in its own special wrapper/...

LYNN *(continuing his rhythm)* ...It looks so easy!/ It
looks like fun!

ELAINE We've taken the worry from working/ we've
laid out what you say and you do./ You must
follow Kwik-Bitey's' fool proof system/ It's all
tried and tested and true.

JOE A dog with hands could do this job.

ELAINE I beg your pardon?

JOE Nothing.

ELAINE No, I want to know what you said!

SUSAN *(quickly)* Hey... here comes the burger.

MARIA *(presenting the burger to SUSAN)* Straights up!

SUSAN Mr. KwikGuest? *(JOE puts on his mask)* Have a nice day.

ELAINE Stop the clock. Two minutes, forty seconds.

> *She takes the burger from JOE and gives it to LYNN.*

LYNN Wow. Thanks.

JOE *(sotto to Susan)* What a dork.

ELAINE So, how does it compare with burgers you've eaten elsewhere?

LYNN Burgers are burgers, I guess.

ELAINE Right, Lynn, that's why we don't sell taste. Gang, tell her what we sell?

**JOE &
SUSAN** S.O.S.

ELAINE *(to LYNN)* Do you know what S.O.S. stands for?

LYNN Like "Help"? If you're out in a boat or something... "Save our Souls"?

**JOE,
SUSAN
&
MARIA** Speed of Service! *(in rhythm)* If you're a mother who's too tired/ Or a traveller running late./ The food may not be gourmet/ but you never have to wait.

Sound. Cars, doors opening, footsteps, conversation. A crowd of customers.

SUSAN   *(warning)* The movie's out!

ELAINE   Pre-cook twelve straights please.

JOE   Thank you.

Sound. A montage of recorded orders, whirring of exhaust fans, sizzling beef, shake makers, bells, whistles and buzzes from other devices under.

ELAINE   Let's go, gang!

SUSAN   *(to customer)* Have a nice day. *(to kitchen)* Three fries.

JOE is flipping and MARIA is assembling burgers, double time from the event before. She shoves the burgers to SUSAN who bags them and gives them to the imaginary customers.

JOE   Thank you.

SUSAN   Have a nice day. *(to kitchen)* Big one, no cheese.

ELAINE   Lynn, put on your hat!

JOE   Thank you.

SUSAN   May I take your order, please.

ELAINE   Now, go, go, go!

LYNN hesitates, then dives in and aces the smile.

LYNN   *(sticking the hat on)* And will you have fries with that?

SUSAN   Have a nice day.

Sound. Sting. The rush is over. Everyone slumps relaxed.

ELAINE *(rousing herself, to SUSAN, JOE and MARIA)* Don't stop. If there's time to lean, there's time to clean. *(she sets an example by wiping a surface as she speaks to LYNN)* Kid, you're going to have your picture up there *(pointing to the billboard)* in no time.

JOE I've never been employee of the month.

MARIA May I go to bathroom now?

ELAINE Well, if you have to, but don't be long. *(continuing to LYNN, as MARIA scurries off)* Lynn, you can take over the counter. *(turning to SUSAN)* Susan, I'm moving you to dining room hostess.

SUSAN *(protesting)* Elaine...

ELAINE I'm sorry, you just won't smile enough. *(she exits)*

LYNN Dining room hostess... that sounds great.

SUSAN takes or mimes a cloth and mop and begins cleaning.

JOE In English that's floor washer and toilet scrubber.

LYNN Oh...

SUSAN Don't worry about it.

LYNN I'll tell her I won't do it. I mean it, Susan.

MARIA runs back on.

SUSAN *(shrugging)* She'd only find someone else.

LYNN It's totally not fair if I take your job.

SUSAN   Lynn, you're replacing a guy who worked here
three years... until he talked back to Elaine.

LYNN   But she seems... kinda nice.

MARIA   Before. *(looking at her)* Before she was nice.
Not now.

JOE   Not since they sent her to Burger U.

LYNN   What's that?

JOE   Kwik-Bitey's has these courses for managers.
Elaine just got promoted.

SUSAN   *(to the point)* Look, whatever job I'm doing, the
money's the same. And in six months I can
apply for a Kwikscholarship.

LYNN   They'll give you a scholarship?

SUSAN   If Elaine recommends me. I can't afford to
make waves.

> *Sound. Bridge.*

JOE   Red crew's here.

> *JOE and MARIA put the leftover burgers in a
bag.*

LYNN   You don't throw those away, do you?

JOE   We have to leave them for the boss to count.

SUSAN   She throws them away.

LYNN   Shouldn't they be given to the homeless, or
something?

SUSAN   *(exasperated)* Lynn...

MARIA   Smiles are free.

SUSAN   But only smiles.

        MARIA puts containers etc. in a garbage bag.

LYNN   We could at least recycle the paper.

SUSAN   *(really exasperated)* Lynn! Chill!

JOE   *(in unison with SUSAN)* Chill!

        JOE starts putting rings and pins back on.

LYNN   So... Susan, I have the car if you want a ride.

SUSAN   *(shaking her head)* I'm meeting someone.

LYNN   Someone... like Jerry?

JOE   Jerry, eh? Who's Jerry?

SUSAN   Bug off.

LYNN   *(to MARIA)* How about you? Would you like a drive home?

MARIA   *(to LYNN)* Yes, please. Thank you.

JOE   I could use a lift. *(LYNN hesitates)* I wouldn't ask but my mom's waiting to unload my kid.

LYNN   *(incredulous)* You have a kid?

JOE   *(defensively)* What's the matter with that?

LYNN   Nothing... it's just I didn't think of you being married, that's all.

SUSAN   *(warning)* Lynn.

JOE   Who said I was married?

LYNN   Oh. Well, sure I can drive you.

JOE turns away to pick up his gear.

MARIA *(to LYNN)* His woman—run away.

LYNN She left her baby?

SUSAN Shh.

LYNN With him?

JOE Ready?

ELAINE *(entering)* Gang, we're short a crew member. Would you stay on, please... Joe?

JOE Gee, Elaine...

ELAINE Last week you were begging for extra hours.

JOE Yeah, like if I know a bit in advance, eh?

ELAINE *(turning to SUSAN)* Susan?

SUSAN *(pause)* Elaine, really, any other night I'd be glad to...

LYNN *(jumping in)* I can stay.

ELAINE You're not trained on grill yet. *(turning to MARIA)* Maria, I'm sure I can count on you?

MARIA *(by rote)* Yes, Elaine. Thank you.

ELAINE exits.

LYNN *(after her)* Elaine... *(but she's gone, then to SUSAN)* I forgot to ask what the pay was?

SUSAN Take a guess.

ALL   Everyone's disposable
             That's the order of the day
             When unemployment is at maximum
             You're content with minimum pay.

SUSAN   There are kids who save for college

LYNN   Or to buy the latest rage

ALL   There's a line up at the counter
             For jobs at minimum wage.

JOE   There are men who worked in factories
             Till their jobs migrated south,

MARIA   There's an army of weary women
             Who are living hand to mouth.

ALL   KwikJobs are dull and boring,
             But you're in out of the rain,
             Though every job leads nowhere,
             And every job's the same.

             Minding machines month by month
             Will make your brain go numb,
             While you're putting in time at minimum pay
             And waiting for a break to come.

             The actors set up the crew room. This could
             mean simply striking props off the counter. We
             might add seats. JOE and SUSAN exit.

LYNN &
MARIA   Hoping that a break will come.
             Praying that a break will come.

             The date on the board is changed to three months
             later as the song segues to the commercial tune.
             In the crew room.

GRIEVANCES

JOE enters and places a cut out ghetto blaster, on loud. His shirt is unbuttoned. Sound. Some raucous hit-parade tape.

SUSAN *(entering, her hat still in her hand, she changes the date to January)* Maria not here? *(JOE can't hear her, she turns the ghetto blaster down)* Have you seen Maria?

JOE They called her in early... to replace Bob Sung on green crew.

SUSAN Bob sick?

JOE Nope. *(SUSAN looks at him)* Elaine ran out of milk last night. *(buttoning his shirt)* Guess who she found behind the counter at the 7-11?

SUSAN *(pause)* Bummer.

JOE What law says you can't hold down two jobs, eh?

SUSAN Joe, you got something on your shirt.

JOE I didn't make the laundromat.

SUSAN Better ask Elaine to rent you one.

JOE *(explaining his plan)* I get to the grill before she sees me... I say I spilled some grease... like just now.

SUSAN She's still going to make you change.

JOE She lends me a shirt... free.

SUSAN In your dreams.

JOE   She's conned two bucks out of me so far this week.

SUSAN   I know, but—

JOE   I lost my name tag. Seventy-five cents. She fined me for smoking in the parking lot. That cap for the softball game against Wendy's...

LYNN enters in time to hear soft ball game.

LYNN   That was fun. *(they look at her)* Well, I scored three hits.

JOE   I had to pay a whole dollar for the cap!

LYNN   Yeah... but the money's for a good cause.

JOE   What about my cause? 'Cause I earn my money and I want to take it home.

SUSAN   Going up there in a dirty uniform is asking for a bad scene.

LYNN   Where's Maria?

SUSAN points upward.

JOE   What's all this about Maria?

LYNN   We're supposed to meet her... a half-hour before our shift.

SUSAN   *(to LYNN)* Hey, you didn't tell us — how did your three month evaluation go?

LYNN   Elaine heard me offer some customer a packet of ketchup.

JOE   *(laughing)* There goes your shot at employee of the month.

SUSAN *(mimicking the boss)* You must learn to think globally. If every hostess in every Kwik-Bitey's gave away more condiments than she was asked for...

JOE Our profits would drop to only seven-hundred billion zillion a year.

> *MARIA enters. SUSAN goes to switch radio stations.*

LYNN Hi, Maria.

MARIA Sorry, sorry.

RADIO HOST ...our caller from Brampton, and what's on your mind?

MARIA *(imitating what's she's just heard on the radio)* And what on your mind?

LYNN *(to MARIA)* "What's". That is short for "what is."

JOE *(turning the radio off)* Get a life.

> *MARIA points to LYNN and SUSAN by way of explanation.*

MARIA I learn—I am learning English.

LYNN Joe, we're helping Maria practice.

SUSAN *(to JOE)* You get outta bed on the wrong side this morning?

JOE I'm tired, that's all.

SUSAN The baby still waking you up?

JOE She's got a tooth coming...

MARIA   Tooth?

SUSAN   *(pointing to one of hers)* Tooth. Baby tooth.

MARIA   Oh... *(understanding, to JOE)* She cry all night.

LYNN   I remember baby-sitting my niece—

JOE   *(over her)* I thought it was a fever, so I took her to "emerge." The nurses looked at me like I was a Klingon. How was I supposed to know, eh?

SUSAN   Why didn't you call your mother?

JOE   'Cause I'm calling her all the time. And she's got problems of her own. *(pause)* Cause she thinks I'm crazy. The nurses think I'm crazy. Maybe I am crazy.

SUSAN   I don't think you're crazy.

JOE   But if I give her up... Mom was telling me you can choose now... I could pick her out a doctor or a lawyer... or one of those rich computer types.

SUSAN   A nerd? *(JOE shrugs)* I'd hate having a nerd for a father.

JOE   Even a rich one?

SUSAN   Oh, yeah. I bet she'd hate it too.

JOE   Maybe. Yeah. *(cheering up)* She'd hate it. *(ELAINE enters with a typed schedule which she can tape on the billboard)* Oh, Elaine, I need to rent a shirt.

ELAINE   In a minute. *(to everyone)* Gang, we're falling below company standard on fry yield. There'll be a bonus for the first shift that hits the target.

She starts off. MARIA takes a quick glance at the schedule.

MARIA   *(coming forward)* Elaine... me... I... on grill all the time?

SUSAN   You promised her some time on the counter?

JOE goes to the schedule.

ELAINE   *(as in "get real")* Susan...

LYNN   Her comprehension's great. She just shy about speaking...

SUSAN   Maria, show her.

MARIA   *(virtually accentless)* Welcome to our restaurant. May I take your order please?

ELAINE   That's quite an improvement, Maria.

MARIA   Will you have fries with that?

ELAINE   Unfortunately, the problem isn't your accent... *(carefully)* It's company policy... our guests expect a certain image.

SUSAN   Like "cute"?

ELAINE   Like happy. Fun. Young.

JOE   *(reacting to the schedule)* What the hell...

ELAINE   Watch your language, please.

JOE   You marked me down for three-and-a-half hours.

SUSAN rushes to look at the schedule, followed by MARIA.

JOE   I'm not a part timer, eh? I do a minimum of six.

SUSAN   We've only got seventeen hours for the whole
         week. I mean... that's all anybody has... total!

MARIA   Mistake, yes? Mistake?

ELAINE   I'm sorry, Maria. *(to everybody)* Kwik-Bitey's
         has decided that the staff must look fresh all the
         time. We can't have tired, irritable employees
         around our guests.

JOE   When was I irritable? Tell me when?

LYNN   *(warning)* Joe...

MARIA   *(with a touch of panic)* I never tired. Never.

ELAINE   Maria, it's nothing personal. We need you to be
         on your toes... to look like you're having fun.

JOE   Hey Maria... I'm on my toes. *(twirling her
         around)* We're KwikHappy / we're
         KwikSnappy—

ELAINE   You're insubordinate!

         Silence.

JOE   Elaine, look... please... five days of three-and-a-
         half hours. That's around a hundred bucks.

ELAINE   You'll still get discounts on food. *(JOE bangs the
         table and turns away)* Joe, I won't put up with
         this.

JOE   I been working here for two lousy years.

LYNN   *(cautiously)* It doesn't seem very fair. I mean
         it's okay for Susan and me, but—

SUSAN   Not for me. My mother's lost her job, remem-
         ber.

JOE   I can't make it on a hundred... there's no way.

ELAINE It's a new directive from the head office. I'm sorry, but there's nothing I can do. Now, *(glancing at the clock or her watch)* You're on deck in five. Oh... Maria, you've already done four hours. I have to send you home. *(she exits)*

LYNN I cannot believe this. It's so... simply unfair.

JOE I'd do better on pogey.

SUSAN You won't get unemployment if you quit. Not for ages anyway.

LYNN *(full of sympathy for JOE)* It's absolutely not fair.

JOE *(taking out his anger on her)* Will you stop saying that!

LYNN Well, it isn't. And somebody should do something!

JOE Yeah, missy prissy? Like who?

SUSAN Don't call her that.

JOE Okay, you tell me who's going to do something?

SUSAN I don't know...

JOE Nobody! 'Cause Elaine says "it's my way or the highway." And there's nothing anybody can do. Absolutely sweet stinking nothing. *(he exits)*

LYNN *(to MARIA)* Don't worry, Maria... it'll be all right.

> *LYNN exits. SUSAN stands, looking at MARIA. She touches her shoulder before exiting. MARIA exits.*

TAKING ACTION

LYNN is walking home. SUSAN runs after her. Both are out of uniform.

SUSAN   Lynn... wait up?

LYNN   I thought you'd be meeting Jerry.

SUSAN   He's studying for French. Where's your car?

LYNN   Home. I'm walking off the fat I eat here.

SUSAN   Listen, I was thinking about Joe and Maria... and about Bob Sung too.

LYNN   The guy who got fired?

SUSAN   Yeah. Like Joe said, there's no law against having two part time jobs.

LYNN   No law at all.

SUSAN   And... well... I was thinking about my mother... *(LYNN winces)* Your dad had to pay her a severance, right?

LYNN   He manages the place. He doesn't own it.

SUSAN   Yeah, but he couldn't just say... "You're out of here," like Elaine did to Bob.

LYNN   Dad's not a mean person. Honestly, Susan, he's not.

SUSAN   Okay, okay. But when the rumours started... that there were going to be lay offs... I remember mom saying, "At least we have a union. We'll have a bit of protection."

LYNN   (*uncomfortably*) Actually, I don't think dad
            agrees with unions much.

SUSAN   But maybe you could ask him... like what he
            was allowed to do, and what he wasn't?

LYNN   Why don't you ask your mother?

SUSAN   She told me to keep my mind on my scholar-
            ship.

LYNN   What's the point anyway? I mean, we don't
            have a union.

SUSAN   Yeah... except... they started one at Harvey's.

LYNN   Harvey's?

SUSAN   As in McDonald's, Wendy's, KFC, Burger King,
            Kwik-Bitey's? This guy at Harvey's started a
            union. It was in the paper last winter.

LYNN   Susan... don't even think about it.

SUSAN   Why? You said it yourself. Somebody has to
            do something.

LYNN   I didn't mean us.

SUSAN   (*shrugging*) Who else is there?

LYNN   The full-time people.

SUSAN   Except there aren't any after today, remember?

LYNN   Okay, I mean adults.

SUSAN   Most of the adults who work here are like Joe
            or Maria. They're kinda at a disadvantage.

LYNN   Okay... but... was the guy who started the union
            at Harvey's still in high school?

SUSAN   I don't remember. But maybe I should make
        like it's a school project and hit the library.

        SUSAN and LYNN exit.

REACTION

*From a different direction JOE and MARIA enter
the break room. MARIA changes the date on the
board to a week later.*

JOE   *(imitating Nicholson's HOFFA)* "Put down that
        bleep bleep burger, you bleep bleeper!" You see
        that movie?

MARIA   *(reacting in fear)* I don't want fight... I don't
        want strike.

        LYNN enters, buttoning her uniform top.

LYNN   I guess Susan's been talking to you about her
        idea?

JOE   She's been talking to everybody, eh? All week.

LYNN   So, like—what do people on the other shifts
        think?

        SUSAN enters in uniform.

JOE   Oh, you know...
        Unions are run by the mafia./
        If you judge by Hollywood./
        They're full of low riff raff—

MARIA   Eee—ah./

JOE   Who needs a bunch of hoods?/

SUSAN   Did you guys ever see "Norma Rae", or
"Silkwood" or "Matewan?" *(they all shake their
heads)* Well, rent a movie and check out the
other side of the story.

LYNN   I guess there's good and bad people in unions,
just like there is in management.

SUSAN   Way back in a bygone age
Working days were twelve hours long
Even children slaved for starvation wages
And no one called it wrong.
But workers struggled to unite
Or it still would be that way
Unions fought for every right
Most folks enjoy today.

JOE   Hey, that's crappola.

SUSAN   No, I looked it up... unions won the right to
have pensions, and sick benefits, and safe
working conditions... or compensation if you
do get hurt on the job. Like the right to have a
vacation with pay. Like the right not to be
shoved around just because the boss is in a bad
mood. Like the right to be treated as if you
counted for something instead of like you were
dirt.

LYNN   That sounds like propaganda to me.

SUSAN   I'm not asking you to take my word. I'm asking you to check it out for yourself.

LYNN   But even if what you're saying is true... like
Dad says "That was then. This is now."
Ancient history's a sedative/
This is the nineties, eh?/
You have to be competitive./

SUSAN   Or so experts always say./

LYNN   Put collective bargains on the shelf./

JOE   Who wants to share slim pickin's?/
            It's every man for himself—/

LYNN   Or herself...

SUSAN   As the elephant tells the chickens.

LYNN   What you have to understand is that we are in
            a post-industrial economy.

SUSAN   Yeah, but what does that mean?

LYNN   It means anyone who's got a job, even a tempo-
            rary job, is really lucky.

SUSAN   Look, guys—I don't understand much about
            economics and all that—but it makes sense to
            me that—well—as long as it's a great big com-
            pany against Joe, or Maria or you or me...
            well... none of us has a chance, right? But if we
            had an organisation that could go to bat for us...
            well... we might have a chance—that's all.

JOE   Chill!

            ELAINE enters with an "audit type" form.

ELAINE Did anyone eat any burgers without writing it
            down?

            MARIA shakes her head nervously.

JOE   Not me.

ELAINE Who put the waste in the bag?

JOE   I did...

ELAINE How many patties?

JOE   I don't remember... four or five, maybe.

ELAINE There was one when I looked this morning.

JOE   *(looking at the floor)* Like I said, I don't remember.

        MARIA shakes her head.

ELAINE   There's nearly a pound-and-a-half of meat unaccounted for. Joe, you know stealing food is instant dismissal?

JOE   Elaine, I swear... I didn't take so much as a chip.

ELAINE   This better not happen again. *(she stares at him for a long beat)* Or you're outta here. *(pause)* Lynn, you were short on cash... two dollars and forty cents.

LYNN   This guy ordered, and then—

ELAINE   *(cutting her off)* The money will be deducted from your next cheque.

        ELAINE exits.

JOE   Bitch. *(to SUSAN)* So, about this union... how do I sign up?

SUSAN   We have to find one to join first.

LYNN   Hey, guys, slow down—

JOE   *(to SUSAN)* You find one.

SUSAN   No, this is something we should all do together.

LYNN   Look, I admit Elaine is being unfair—

JOE   *(cutting her off, to SUSAN)* You're the one who knows about this stuff. You get it going, I'll sign up.

SUSAN   *(hesitating)* Okay. *(exiting)* I'll get back to you.

        JOE follows her off.

MARIA *(calling after her)* No, Susan, please, no.

LYNN Maria, nobody has to get involved if they don't want to, you know.

MARIA You are nice girl, Lynn. But you understand nothing.

> *MARIA exits. LYNN stands a moment, then follows her. Sound. Bridge.*

ORGANISING

> *SUSAN's home. The date is changed to the next day. SUSAN enters, out of uniform, with a portable phone tucked under her ear, a list of numbers in one hand and a pencil or pen in the other.*

SUSAN *(into the phone)* Me? I'm seventeen. *(pause)* But what difference... *(pause)* Oh. Does that go for all unions?

> *LYNN enters, out of uniform.*

SUSAN *(pause)* Okay. *(automatically)* Have a nice day.

LYNN Your mother let me in.

SUSAN Yeah?

LYNN Dad had this party and there was all these leftovers... so I suggested I'd drive it all to the Food Bank...

SUSAN So...

LYNN Maria was there... with her four little kids. They were picking up stuff. So—I guess if you're willing to risk your scholarship...

SUSAN   I don't want to, but I can't let Kwik-Bitey's treat
          Joe and Maria this badly.

LYNN   I can't either. I just hope dad never finds out.

SUSAN   *(giving her the slip of paper)* Call out the num-
          bers. I'm at the fifth one down.

LYNN   747-6051. *(SUSAN punches in the phone number)*

SUSAN   *(into the phone)* Hi, I want to speak to a union
          organiser.

LYNN   So all the crossed out ones said no?

SUSAN   Yeah. *(into the phone)* Fast food. *(pause)* Part-
          time. ...Yeah, grade 12. ...Seventeen, but listen...
          (pause) Right. Have a nice day. *(to LYNN)*
          Next?

LYNN   1-800-265-2189. You know, I wish you'd stop
          saying "Have a nice day."

SUSAN   I didn't, did I?

LYNN   You do all the time. Even in school.

SUSAN   You're kidding— *(into the phone)* Hi, Hello.
          May I speak with an organiser, please? *(to
          LYNN)* Do I really?

LYNN   I did it to Mr. Wachuk after English. He said
          "Sorry, I've made other plans."

SUSAN   Jerry says he can't tell if I'm smiling because of
          him, or... *(into the phone)* Oh, yes. I'm looking
          for information on how to join your union.
          (pause) Why do you ask that? *(pause)* Oh, I
          have a young voice, that's all. Actually, I'm
          quite old really.

LYNN   Susan!

SUSAN   A committee? *(she gives the high sign to LYNN)*
        Yes, as a matter of fact we have—just now—
        formed a committee. *(pause)* On all shifts?
        ...ah... about sixty-two. But that would include
        the boss and *(pause)* ...not the managers?

LYNN   Minus Elaine and... three assistants. Fifty-eight.

SUSAN   The committee secretary says we have fifty-
        eight workers. *(pause)* Mine? What for?
        (pause) Oh, oh, great! 2910 Markdale Drive.
        M9Z 4Y2. Thanks. Have a—I mean, good bye.

LYNN   What's happening?

SUSAN   He's sending us a guidelines package!

LYNN   Then... we'll have a union?

SUSAN   All we have to do is sign up fifty-five percent of
        all the guys who work at the franchise... fifty-
        five percent of fifty-eight?

LYNN   *(reaching into her purse)* The secretary requires
        her calculator.

SUSAN   We're going to need everybody's phone num-
        ber. You'll have to get the master list and pho-
        tocopy it.

LYNN   *(looking up from her calculator)* Me?

SUSAN   Say you want to send out party invitations or
        something. *(seeing LYNN'S face)* Elaine likes
        you... she won't suspect anything.

LYNN   Can't we just ask for a list?

SUSAN   Listen, if the boss finds out about this, we're
        hamburger.

        Sound. The phone rings. They both jump.

LYNN   It's not possible.

SUSAN   (*nervously*) Hello... (*relieved*) Oh, Jerry, I'll call
        you back, okay? (*pause*) Because I'm real busy.
        (*small pause*) I'll tell you about it later. Gotta
        go. (*hanging up, then to LYNN*) So, what's the
        magic number?

LYNN   Thirty-one point nine.

LYNN   Thirty-one point nine.

SUSAN   Point nine? I guess that's Joe! (*they laugh*) Hey,
        hey, Lynn... we can do this thing! (*they run off*)

        Sound. Musical bridge.

SIGNING UP

        *MUSIC under a choreographed, stylised section
        as JOE turns the billboard to reveal the score-
        board. The teams are now designated "YES" and
        "NO." ELAINE changes the date. MARIA
        passes out hand-held masks which they hold
        before their faces and create personalities—like
        real fast—as LYNN and SUSAN enter and dash
        about persuading people to sign cards.*

SUSAN   (*offering a card*) Sign for dignity, respect...

MASK   Can we take a leak without asking? (*YES: 1*)

COOL
MASK   A union is something... I might picture myself
        joining... if I were like... dead. (*NO: 1*)

        *During the rest of the dialogue the scoreboard is
        changed by the actors with the NO side taking
        the lead.*

LYNN   Sign for more fair treatment.

MASK   How about better wages?

LYNN   *(uncertain)* For sure.

SUSAN   Well... we can negotiate a contract... *(YES: 7)*

MASK   Sounds great.

LYNN   *(to another)* They won't be able to fire you.

SUSAN   Not without just cause.

MASK   I guess I'm just not a labour sort of person.

LYNN   You work here.

MASK   It's only temporary. *(NO: 11)*

SUSAN   *(to another)* Sure, there are dues, *(NO: 13)* but not very much when you consider. *(YES: 10)*

COOLEST
MASK   Not. *(NO:16)*

LYNN   Why not?

COOLER
MASK   Because *(elegantly gesturing)* I live in the world.

SUSAN   *(to another)* Seniority will count.

The YES side of the scoreboard starts to catch up.

LYNN   *(to another)* You've heard of empowerment, haven't you?

MASK   The bosses aren't going to give us anything unless we show strength. *(YES: 14)*

SUSAN   *(to another)* Sign here and we'll have input into scheduling.

The numbers on the YES side mount quickly.

MASK   Things couldn't get worse. *(YES: 21)*

MASK   My old man was a miner. He says the union saved his life.

MASK   It's good you're doing this. Thank you. *(YES: 33)*

CHORUS   Thank you, Susan. We're with you all the way.

> *The scoreboard flips to: YES: 42. NO: 16.*

SUSAN   Forty-two out of fifty-eight!

LYNN   That's more than fifty-five percent.

SUSAN   *(jumping up and down)* We did it!

> *Sound. Cheers.*

JOE   We have our union?

SUSAN   We send in the cards, the labour board certifies us, then we have our union!

LYNN   It's a piece of cake!

SUSAN   It's a big one with cheese!

LYNN   Watch out, Kwik-Bitey's!

SUSAN   We're going to make things better for everybody.

LYNN   After the shift... let's go celebrate.

JOE   I'm broke.

SUSAN   You'll have more money soon.

LYNN   My treat for now.

JOE   Yea, Susan... yea, Lynn.

*All sing a high-spirited rendition of one verse of
"Solidarity Forever," during which the break
room props are removed and the restaurant
restored. The date is changed to three days later.
June. LYNN and SUSAN don full uniform.
Before the last few words, ELAINE enters. Big
silence. LYNN, JOE, SUSAN and MARIA take
their places for work.*

<u>DISCOVERY</u>

LYNN   Welcome to our restaurant. May I take your
order, please?

    *Sound. Taped orders, and the noises of the
machines at a fairly slow pace.*

ELAINE   Susan, you're on the counter. Lynn...

    *She beckons to LYNN. LYNN and SUSAN
exchange a glance as LYNN follows ELAINE to a
corner.*

    Lynn, you're one of the best workers I ever had
here...

LYNN   Oh, I... thanks.

ELAINE   You're intelligent, enthusiastic... and you're
popular.

LYNN   Thanks.

ELAINE   So tell me, why is there a sudden silence every
time I appear?

LYNN   Oh... is there?

ELAINE   *(disappointed)* Lynn.

LYNN   Well, I mean... you can't blame people for being
upset.

ELAINE Who's upset? Are you?

LYNN Well, no... I mean... three-and-a-half hour shifts are perfect for me.

ELAINE Susan?

LYNN Well... she really needs to save, you know.

ELAINE Do you think some more activities would help? A party... a scavenger hunt?

LYNN I don't know.

ELAINE I'd really value your opinion.

LYNN Well... if you really would...

ELAINE Yes?

LYNN Don't take offence... but scavenger hunts are kinda childish. I mean... Joe and Maria aren't exactly—like in grade one.

ELAINE Joe and Maria. So, they're the ones complaining?

LYNN No! I only used their names because they're on my team. But they have families to provide for. You realise Joe is a single parent, don't you?

ELAINE So am I.

LYNN You?

ELAINE I've been providing for two daughters by myself for eleven years.

LYNN Oh...

ELAINE   Joe's not the only person that ever got dumped, Lynn. My husband walked out after the second kid. And I didn't even have a mother to babysit for me.

LYNN   Yeah... but you know, some people are better at coping than others.

ELAINE   Some people work at being better. I started on crew at a place like this and I worked my butt off. I went to all the social stuff, I canvassed for the charities, I did everything I was asked and a whole lot more. I got to be shift leader in six months, and second assistant manager by the end of my first year.

LYNN   Yeah, but how long were your shifts back then? I mean, Joe can't earn enough to get by...

ELAINE   Lynn, I can't go against company policy. What good would it do anybody if I got fired?

LYNN   Yeah... that's what my dad said...

ELAINE   The thing is—this is my first head management job. If I show a good bottom line, they'll let me into a profit-sharing scheme. I'll be able to buy a franchise of my own. Do you know how many women get to be owners in Kwik-Bitey's system?

LYNN   Not many I guess.

ELAINE   So, woman to woman, Lynn, I could really use a little support. Is there anything going on here I should know about?

LYNN   *(pause)* Elaine, maybe you should talk to all the guys the way you just talked to me...

ELAINE   You think Joe would care about my problems? It really rots his socks to have a female for a boss.

LYNN No. He's just scared. He's afraid he's not good
      enough to be a father. Maybe he's not smart,
      but he tries. *(softer, because she sees Elaine is lis-*
      tening) You know, I bet... if you encourage him
      a little... inspire him even... I bet he'd love to be
      your friend.

ELAINE *(realising she means it)* You think so? *(pause)*
        Perhaps you're right.

        Having made a decision, she wastes no time
        implementing it.

        (to JOE) Joe... in my office. *(JOE follows her off)*

SUSAN *(lingering by the counter, as LYNN joins her)*
       What did she say?

LYNN I feel like a sleazebag. *(to a customer)* May I
      take your order please?

SUSAN Lynn?

LYNN And will you have apple pie with that?

       Sound. Repeat the "movies out" sound cue.

LYNN The movie's out. *(to the kitchen)* Ten straights,
      please.

MARIA Where's Joe?

SUSAN Does she suspect?

LYNN *(to a customer)* Have a nice day. *(to another)*
      Welcome to our restaurant. *(to the kitchen)* Two
      fries, please.

       MARIA is over-taxed trying to grill and assem-
       ble and fry.

MARIA Susan!

LYNN   *(gesturing towards the kitchen)* Susan...

SUSAN   Lynn, tell me what she said?

LYNN   Later. Go help Maria will you?

> *MARIA screams. She's burned her hand. LYNN rushes to MARIA.*

SUSAN   First aid box!

JOE   *(reappearing)* What's happening?

ELAINE   *(following JOE)* Is she hurt?

MARIA   Okay. Not bad.

LYNN   It could get infected.

ELAINE   *(to the imaginary customers)* We'll be with you in a moment. *(to MARIA)* Let me see.

SUSAN   *(with the first aid box)* Two lousy Band-Aids!

ELAINE   *(to LYNN)* She'd better go to the hospital. Go, hail a taxi. *(to SUSAN, as she positions MARIA out of the way)* Get her things from her locker. *(to JOE)* Take over the grill. *(to a customer, with a totally charming smile)* I apologise for the disruption. May I take your order, please?

> *Sound. A montage of high pitched activity.*

ELAINE   *(to customers)* Have a nice day. May I take your order please? And will you have fries with that? May I take your order, please? *(to JOE)* Great work. Keep it up.

JOE   *(with genuine admiration)* Way to go, boss.

LYNN   *(reappearing)* Come on, Maria.

> *Sound. Sting. The rush is over.*

> SUSAN appears with a bag which ELAINE takes
> from her.

MARIA   (protesting as LYNN guides her to the door) I
        okay... okay.

ELAINE It's all right. I'll pay you for the day.

> As ELAINE escorts MARIA off, she notices
> something about the feel of the bag. She peeks
> into it before handing it to MARIA.

LYNN   Red crew's on.

JOE   (coming off grill) You seen the way the boss han-
        dled that rush?

ELAINE (smiling at him) With your help. We make a
        great team, eh, Joe? (to everybody) In fact, we
        all make a great team.

SUSAN   Uh, oh.

ELAINE I suppose it must seem like I forget that some-
        times, but guys, listen up.

        Maybe I've been inflexible
        But that was yesterday
        Now, there's going to be some changes
        And you're all going to have your say.

        I won't yell or nag or put you down
        You'll find working here okay
        I'll make sure you have SIX hours
        And take—

JOE   Six?

ELAINE And take home a lot more pay.

JOE   Way to go!

SUSAN   (to LYNN) You told her!

LYNN   No!

SUSAN   She's found out somehow. She must have!

ELAINE   That you're trying to cause a lot of trouble around here? Oh, yes, Susan, I've found out.

SUSAN   *(to ELAINE)* It wasn't just me, Elaine. Everybody voted for the union.

ELAINE   Everybody?

LYNN   Almost everybody.

SUSAN   Forty-two out of fifty-five signed. It's too late to start being nice now.

ELAINE   Actually, I understand you're not certified yet?

SUSAN   We will be! There's nothing you can do to stop it!

ELAINE   Watch me.

> *Sound. Sting. ELAINE hands JOE a letter. JOE steps forward.*

JOE   Dear Labour Board, I am writing to you of my own free will to tell you I was tricked into signing a union card.

SUSAN   Joe!

JOE   The whole thing was started by a couple of trouble makers who promised us big wage hikes and that we'd be able to dick ...dicket...

ELAINE   Dictate.

JOE   To dictate our own hours.

SUSAN   We never said that.

LYNN   She only said we'd have input.

JOE   *(pointing to LYNN)* She offered to take me out drinking if we signed.

SUSAN   That's a lie!

ELAINE   You said you'd treat him to a celebration. Do you deny that?

LYNN   But that was after he signed.

JOE   *(pointing to SUSAN)* She never told us the union would take half our wages.

SUSAN   Eighteen cents an hour isn't half.

JOE   *(continuing)* Things are okay around here. We don't want a union. We don't need a union. Please don't certify one in this great place.

ELAINE   If anyone else wants to sign Joe's letter, we could put a stop to this stupid idea right now.

SUSAN   No one is going to sign a bunch of lies like that.

JOE   *(to the audience)* Just say no, okay? *(he passes out buttons)*

SUSAN   *(to everybody)* Can't you see what's happened? Elaine made Joe write that letter!

JOE   Just say no.

SUSAN   *(to everybody)* Don't sign it. Please, don't sign it!

LYNN   *(a quieter moment to ELAINE)* Elaine, why are you being so mean?

ELAINE   My girls aren't going to Hamburger U. They'll
go to a real university, just like you. But if this
Union happens, I'm finished at Kwik-Bitey's.
That's why I have to stop you and Susan, and
stop you I will.

> *JOE comes to her and proudly presents her with
> the letter.*

JOE   Thirteen of the guys changed their minds, boss.

> *ELAINE walks to the scoreboard and changes it.
> YES: 29. NO: 29.*

ELAINE   You need fifty-five percent to be certified,
Susan? You don't seem to have that anymore.

> *LYNN and SUSAN turn their backs on JOE and
> ELAINE and all freeze. Sound. Bridge.*

COUNTER ATTACK

JOE   *(coming out of freeze and producing a letter)* Hey,
Gang! We got a reply from the Labour Board.
(not certain of its legalese) I think we stopped the
union.

SUSAN   *(coming out of freeze)* I don't believe it!

ELAINE   *(coming out of freeze, taking the letter from JOE and
scanning it)* Because so many people wrote that
Susan and Lynn intimidated them into signing
union cards, the Labour Board refuses to certify
a union in this franchise at this time.

> *SUSAN grabs letter from ELAINE and scans it.*

LYNN   *(coming out of freeze)* But that's not fair!

SUSAN   Wait! It's not over! They want us to have a
vote! A secret vote! It's going to be right here,
next Saturday!

ELAINE Joe, we start campaigning right now!

LYNN *(to SUSAN)* What are we going to do?

SUSAN Start phoning again! Look, there were twenty-nine guys who didn't sign Joe's letter... that means they still want the union. All we need is thirty-one votes...

LYNN Thirty-one point nine.

SUSAN Thirty-two then... we just have to convince three people to switch back to our side again.

> *MARIA brings on the phone to SUSAN and the ghettoblaster to ELAINE. Sound. The radio talk-show.*

HOST Our next caller is from the greater metro area... and what's on your mind, ma'am?

CALLER *(who might sound a lot like ELAINE)* Kids today! Can you believe that Susan Carter trying to form a union at Kwik-Bitey's?

HOST What's with that girl? Doesn't she know the Soviet Union went belly up? The free ride is over, baby. If you expect your Doc Martins delivered to you on a silver platter, forget it! You know what you are, Susan. You're a KwikBrat.

JOE Right on!

> *Sound. Catcalls. Cries of "Commie scum" "KwikBrat." SUSAN sinks to the floor. Everybody except SUSAN exits.*

FALL OUT

SUSAN punches in a number on the phone.

SUSAN   Is Bill there, please? *(pause)* Well, would you tell him Susan Carter— *(pause)* the paper? No, I haven't had time. *(pause)* Mrs. Katzin, I'm not a communist. I just— *(a hang up, she sighs, then punches another number)* Marion, look, I wanted to talk to you about why you changed your mind... yeah, it's Susan... *(pause)* No, what are they saying? *(pause)* That's really dumb! I mean, what does starting a union have to do with whether I get dates or not? Anyway I've got Jerry. *(pause)* No, I couldn't go to the concert. I was working on this union stuff, which is why I'm phoning— *(pause)* Karen Harris? *(pause)* No, no. I'm not upset. I mean, he did ask me first... listen, Marion, my mom's calling... I'll see you tomorrow, okay? *(she hangs up, hesitates then punches in another number)* Jerry? Hi. *(pause)* I know, I been kinda busy... *(pause)* Wanta go to a movie or something? *(pause)* Oh... well, could I come over for a bit? I'm kinda down and I just need some one to talk to... *(pause)* Oh. *(challenging)* With Karen? *(pause)* Yeah, I heard. So—see ya around I guess. *(she puts down the phone, dejected)*

LYNN   *(entering after a beat)* Susan... you missed that math test today.

SUSAN   Who had time to open a book?

LYNN   You're going to lose your chance for any kind of scholarship.

SUSAN   The way I'm going, I could lose my whole year.

LYNN   You ever think... maybe...

SUSAN What?

LYNN Well, is the union really worth it? I mean, if you hit the books, you could still pass, and even if you don't get a scholarship, at least you still have your job...

SUSAN Oh, yeah? For how long?

LYNN It's against the law for Elaine to fire someone for trying to form a union.

SUSAN So she fires us for having a bad attitude... or wearing too much makeup.

LYNN No... she can't. Dad told her it would look vindictive if she fired you for at least six months.

SUSAN Dad?

LYNN Yeah.

SUSAN Your dad is giving advice to Elaine?

LYNN She came over to our house last night. I think she went to see a lot of parents.

SUSAN Oh, no.

LYNN She told Dad—like how much trouble we were causing her... how hurt she was... and how... it could really be a black mark on my employment record...

SUSAN So... what happened? Did your dad say to lose the union or you lose your car?

LYNN He didn't go ballistic. He just talked to me. He helped me to... you know... get things straight in my mind.

SUSAN Let me guess... like business is business.

LYNN Well, it is... and management has to do what's best for the business. I think Elaine should be allowed to pick her own team. I mean nobody is born with a right to work for her.

SUSAN Nobody's born with a right to anything. It's like the Union pamphlet says... society... that's government and voters and all that... agree to make life more fair for people.

LYNN Yeah... but... there's good and bad on both sides. I just think maybe it's time you sat down with Elaine and talked things over. She really wants to settle this so we won't have to vote tomorrow.

SUSAN Why? What's she scared of?

LYNN She's doesn't want a big deal... more stuff in the paper or on TV.

SUSAN She must think we're going to win.

LYNN That's crazy.

SUSAN Yes... yes, she must. For heaven's sakes, Lynn, think about it... she wouldn't be going to your father unless she was afraid people were going to vote for the union!

LYNN But we don't need one anymore. Susan, listen... she gave Joe and Maria extra shifts, didn't she? She's treating everybody pretty well. I mean, even you have got to admit things are better now.

SUSAN Even me?

LYNN Come on, Susan. You enjoy the confrontation... like... the attention.

SUSAN You think I like people calling me names?

LYNN   Why else are you still fighting when there's no reason to? You do kinda get off on being a star or something.

SUSAN   I don't believe you're saying this to me.

LYNN   I'm sorry, Susan, if you won't listen to reason, I can't help you anymore.

SUSAN   I don't want your help. I don't need it either. *(LYNN exits and SUSAN calls after her)* There's going to be a vote tomorrow, and the union's going to win!

> *SUSAN exits.*

THE VOTE

> *Sound. Bridge segueing to car horns, cat calls from a circus of imaginary onlookers in the parking lot. Chants of "Keep unions away from kids. Hands off our burgers" etc.*
>
> *On stage ELAINE and JOE are also chanting. Sound. The chant outside changes to "KwikBrat, KwikBrat," as SUSAN enters.*

JOE   *(cocky)* Guess you can tell how popular you are, eh?

SUSAN   Let's just do it!

> *Sound. A referee's whistle. JOE changes the scoreboard to 0. 0. MARIA brings on the basketball and there's a toss up between SUSAN and ELAINE. ELAINE wins the toss and the game begins.*

*MARIA changes the score around as ELAINE
and SUSAN hit or miss with their arguments.
JOE leads the canned cheers for ELAINE's side.
LYNN leads the cheering section for SUSAN.
MARIA is always silent. SUSAN and ELAINE
could address the audience as the rest of the crew
dribble and shoot.*

ELAINE Okay. Remember, gang, you can vote yes to
have a union... or no to keep the improvements
I've already made.

SUSAN If you vote no, those improvements won't last
long.

The scoreboard changes. YES: 1. NO: 1.

ELAINE The issue is all about loyalty, you understand.
If you're not loyal to me, you can't expect me to
be loyal to you.

SUSAN *(blocking her)* That's a threat.

ELAINE That's a fact. *(ducking around)* Gang, Kwik-
Bitey's is holding a dinner and dance for all
employees Friday night, and *(shooting)* we've
got the hottest band in town!

*Sound. Cheers. The scoreboard changes. YES:
1. NO: 4.*

SUSAN The money for these parties comes from the
crew fund. We're paying for them ourselves!
(shooting)

*The scoreboard changes. YES: 5. NO: 4. Sound.
Cheers and boos.*

ELAINE Right now, I've a few prizes to give out. For
making the fry yield target... Joe... fifty dollars!

JOE *(thrilled)* Yes!

The scoreboard changes. YES: 5. NO: 10.
Sound. Cheers.

SUSAN   We don't need stupid competitions. We need decent wages. *(shooting)* And she shouldn't be able to make up all the rules. You shouldn't get fired for nothing! And you shouldn't have to suck up to her to get a bonus either!

The scoreboard changes. YES: 11. NO: 10.

ELAINE   I reward the people who deliver! So, gang... tell me what do we sell here?

JOE   S. O. S.

SUSAN   Save our souls.

ELAINE   And because we have the speediest service of any franchise around, we have a brand new free T-shirt for everybody.

The scoreboard changes. YES: 11. NO: 28.

SUSAN   *(running with the ball)* We don't need T-shirts. We need better safety conditions. We need a real first-aid box. *(missing basket)*

ELAINE   Some one forgot to fill it. That was bad. But if Susan had gone to help Maria when she called, we wouldn't have needed a first aid box. *(shooting)*

Sound. Cheers and boos.

SUSAN   *(stopping in the middle of her run and facing the audience)* I mean, use your head, eh? *(throwing the ball away)* This isn't a game. It's all of our futures. If the Union is so bad for us, why is Elaine fighting so hard? Please, guys, try to use your heads!

Sound. Cheers.

ELAINE *(facing the audience)* That's right. Use your heads. Ask yourself why Susan is doing this? She wants to go to college, you all know that. I figure she's made a deal with the union to pay her way.

SUSAN That's not true!

ELAINE You want to know what is true? If you vote for the union, Kwik-Bitey's will close this franchise down. You won't get better wages, you won't get better hours. You'll all lose your jobs... every single one of you!

> *The scoreboard changes. YES: 11. NO: 45. Sound. Cheers.*

ELAINE Well, that's the end of that nonsense.

> *Sound. Wild cheering.*

MARIA Excuse me...

ELAINE Maria?

MARIA I haven't had my turn to vote yet.

ELAINE We wiped the floor with the union side. Your vote can't make any difference.

MARIA I do not care. I have a right.

ELAINE *(shrugging)* Go ahead.

> *MARIA changes the scoreboard to YES: 12.*

SUSAN *(astonished)* Maria!

MARIA I am tired of promises. I am tired of lies. I am tired of threats. *(moving to SUSAN)* You are a brave woman. This way at least I say thank you.

ELAINE   Maria, you're fired.

JOE   *(a protest)* Hey, boss!

SUSAN   You can't!

LYNN   Dad told you! You can't fire people for trying to unionise.

ELAINE   Her dismissal has nothing to do with the way she voted. She's been stealing the leftovers. There were three hamburgers in that bag in her locker.

Silence. MARIA takes off her uniform and exits.

LYNN   But Elaine... I mean you were going to throw them out?

ELAINE   She broke the rules. Now, *(she and JOE turn the scoreboard round to the billboard)* I'll see you and Joe on your next shift.

SUSAN   You'll see me too, Elaine.

ELAINE   You intend to keep working here?

SUSAN   I haven't broken any rules. It's against the law to fire me.

ELAINE   Fine. You can be dining room hostess, permanently.

ELAINE exits. JOE follows ELAINE off.

SUSAN   *(to LYNN)* You didn't even vote, did you?

LYNN   I abstained.

LYNN goes toward the counter, SUSAN makes a move to begin cleaning. They freeze with their backs to each other for a moment.

Sound. Bridge crossfading to whirring of exhaust fans, sizzling beef, shake-makers, bells, whistles and buzzes from other devices.

GOING FORWARD

JOE enters with an "Employee of the Month" picture of himself, which he puts on display before taking his place at the grill.

JOE   *(to SUSAN)* Some kid barfed in the men's washroom.

SUSAN exits wordlessly.

LYNN   *(to JOE)* You could have cleaned it up.

JOE   It's her job.

LYNN   She tried to start that union for you, you know.

JOE   Yeah, because she thinks I'm stupid,—

LYNN   No,—

JOE   —Just like you do. Elaine told me what you said about me. Well, I got news for you. I'm employee of the month this month. If I keep doing good, I'm going to be shift boss. Some day I'm going own a place like this.

ELAINE   *(entering)* Hey, gang. This attempt at unionisation has hurt our image in the community. To compensate, I'm having a car wash for charity Sunday afternoon. I expect every one of you to volunteer.

LYNN   *(a protest)* But Sunday,—

ELAINE   *(continuing over her)* And I want you to wear these new caps. *(producing one)* They only cost two dollars... *(JOE groans)* I'm sorry, but there wasn't enough in the crew fund to pay for that dance band last week. *(SUSAN enters)* Where were you?

SUSAN   In the washroom.

ELAINE   Who gave you permission to go?

JOE   Hey, Elaine...

SUSAN   I was cleaning it, Elaine.

ELAINE   Oh.

LYNN   *(to a customer)* May I take your order, please?

ELAINE   *(going to JOE)* Joe, I have to change your schedule. You can go home at five.

JOE   You promised me six hours!

ELAINE   Starting tomorrow you'll get two shifts.

LYNN   *(to JOE)* Cheeseburger, please.

ELAINE   You can have nine to noon and nine to midnight.

JOE   You're splitting my shifts?

ELAINE   No employee can work more than three hours at a time, remember?

JOE   Yeah, but Elaine...

LYNN   Joe, cheeseburger, please.

JOE   Elaine, you said... *(trying to remember)*

ELAINE   I said six hours. That's three plus three, isn't it?

JOE   My Mom works in the morning.

ELAINE   Joe, Lynn gave you an order.

JOE   Yeah... *(to LYNN)* Thank you. *(to ELAINE)*
             What am I supposed to do with my kid, eh?

ELAINE   There's such a thing as day care.

JOE   Yeah, but there's no way I can pay for it.

ELAINE   I'm not forcing you to take the extra shift.
             There's a line up for jobs, you know. *(JOE slams
             the counter)* One more display of temper like
             that and you're out of here!

LYNN   Elaine... Dad says not being fair to your
             employees isn't good business.

ELAINE   Lynn, there once was a man named Ray Kroc.
             He invented fast food. And what Ray Kroc said
             about business was that it is dog eat dog com-
             petition. The survival of the fittest. I keep fit.
             (she turns to JOE) Take off that pickle! The
             onion goes on first. *(back to LYNN)* Lynn, you
             have a customer, and remember, all of you,
             smiles are free.

LYNN   But only smiles.

JOE   *(to SUSAN)* What are you looking at?

SUSAN   Employee of the month.

JOE   *(thrusting the burger at LYNN)* Just shut up, will
             ya!

LYNN   *(to the customer)* Have a nice day.

SUSAN   Welcome to the KwikWorld
             The World of KwikHappy

LYNN   Where the bosses are KwikCheap

JOE   And working is KwikCrappy.

               They all look at each other, and then manage to share a laugh.

JOE   I guess I've been a whopping big Kwikjerk, eh?

SUSAN Kinda, yeah.

JOE   Okay, okay... so... *(pause)* okay?

SUSAN Okay.

LYNN   Joe, when school's over, I don't have much to do in the mornings... if you brought your daughter in here with you... I could take her to a playground, maybe.

JOE   Would you?

LYNN   Until university starts anyway.

SUSAN Maybe I could too. At least... until... *(she breaks off)*

LYNN   Until you start college?

SUSAN I'm looking for a permanent job for next year.

LYNN   Oh, Susan.

SUSAN I've blown the scholarship. And we all know Elaine is going to get rid of me sooner or later anyway.

LYNN   It's just not fair.

SUSAN Lynn!

LYNN   No, really. It's not just you. She's treating everybody worse than she did before.

JOE   I guess I let her suck me in but good.

SUSAN   Hey, even I thought her improvements would last longer than one week.

LYNN   People are mad at her in a major way. *(SUSAN shrugs)* No, really. A lot of guys are saying how they wish they'd stuck with you. I sure wish I had.

SUSAN   So, why don't you do something about it?

LYNN   Me?

SUSAN   You and Joe, maybe.

LYNN   Susan, I know you got really burned, but... if we do decide to try to unionise again, you will help, won't you?

SUSAN   Yeah, I guess I'd help...

JOE   Like a lot?

SUSAN   Maybe...

LYNN   Because I mean, it's got to be all of us sticking together or there's no point in trying.

SUSAN   Lynn, all of us trying to stick together is the point.

ELAINE   *(off)* If there's time to lean, there's time to clean!

JOE   I think there's going to be a next time.

LYNN   Yeah.

SUSAN   All right!

ALL
THREE   *(to the audience)* So have a nice day.

THE END

Then

and

Now

Then and Now was commissioned by Geordie Theatre
Productions and The Office of the Commissioner of
Official Languages, and was first produced by Geordie
Theatre Productions in 1997.

PEGGY	Marnie Shuster
MARGOT	Michelle Hoisler
DAN	Eric Davis
JACQUES	Ryan Hollyman
AUTHORITY/	
COMPUTER	William Foley

Directed by Elsa Bolam
Set Design	Eo Sharp
Costume Design	Tiffany Oschmann
Lighting	Tim Crack
Stage Manager	Robert Van der Linden

Characters

PEGGY	16
MARGOT	16
DAN	35-40*
JACQUES	35-40*
AUTHORITY/ COMPUTER	ageless

* The age of Dan and Jacques may change to much younger as they take on other characters, or conversely, may be played by younger actors, but made older for the "father" scenes.

Set

A Monopoly board, and one or two large maps. Projections might be used effectively. Minimal props and costume bits are brought on stage in backpacks and sacks as indicated.

Note: A director and designer would benefit from a working knowledge of "Star Trek."

*A background soundscape—nineties city
noises and/or contemporary music. Two girls
enter with back packs. They are unaware of
one another. They each take out a language
text, one French, one English.*

PEGGY   Write a short play—

MARGOT   —une courte pièce—

PEGGY   —on the subject of—

MARGOT   ...la dualité linguistique—

PEGGY   —In Canada.

MARGOT   *(at the same time)* Utilisez votre imagina-
tion.

PEGGY   *(at the same time)* Be creative.

*Each makes a face to indicate bored frustra-
tion.*

PEGGY   I mean, why?

MARGOT   Ah, c'est pas vrai.

PEGGY   I hate this stuff.

MARGOT   *(overlapping PEGGY)* J'haisse ça, ces trucs
là.

*They each toss the books away and eagerly
grab a CD ROM from their packs. They take
up separate places at computer stations and
begin a video deep-space war game.*

> *Sound. A deep-space battle. The girls are shooting down alien ships gleefully. Suddenly, the head of a deep-space humanoid puppet appears.*

PEGGY   Far out!

MARGOT   Génial!

VOICE   *(a triumphant statement)* K'paw Gabong!

MARGOT   Qu'est ce que ça veut dire, ça?

VOICE   K'paw Gabong. Dabak K'swylt.

PEGGY   I don't speak Alienese.

> *Sound. The computer makes an accessing noise.*

VOICE   The universal translator is now activated. On all wavelengths and in all languages... I win, you lose.

MARGOT   Le jeu est pas encore fini.

PEGGY   I've still got shots!

VOICE   Shots are irrelevant. You are inferior. I am superior.

PEGGY   Oh yeah!

MARGOT   *(clicking her mouse)* Je m'en fou, moi.

VOICE   Assimilation is inevitable. Resistance is futile.

> *Two other voices, jaded human males, call from off stage.*

JACQUES   Margot?

DAN	Peggy?
JACQUES	Fais-tu tes devoirs, la?
DAN	Are you studying up there?
MARGOT	Oui p'pa.
PEGGY	*(with MARGOT)* Yes, Dad.
VOICE	That is an untruth in any tongue.

The humanoid throws a Zap toward them. Sound. Zap.

PEGGY	Dad, help!
MARGOT	P'pa! Au secours!

> *The girls freeze in terrified poses for a moment. Then they are dragged by an invisible tractor beam into the computer. Sound. Virtual reality motif.*
>
> *Both dads burst on to the part of the stage occupied by their daughters. The dads are also unaware of each other.*

DAN	What's going on?
JACQUES	*(overlapping)* Qu'est qui s'passe?
VOICE	Accessing your daughters' brains.

> *Sound. The accessing noise. The computer sucks information from the girls' heads.*

DAN	What the—
JACQUES	Mais—

VOICE   Although unknown to each other, Margot
                   and Peggy separately chose the same CD
                   ROM from the video shop so they could
                   goof off on your state of the art systems
                   instead of studying a language which each
                   hates. Therefore—they turned me on.

DAN   It's a hacker!

JACQUES   C'est un virus.

                   The dads try to turn their computers off.

VOICE   I have disabled your control devices... and
                   your escape keys... your power switches are
                   also de-activated. *(as they both reach down)*
                   Attempting to pull the plugs is futile.

                   *Sound. Zap. Another Zap is thrown and the
                   dads freeze and are dragged into the comput-
                   er.*

VOICE   Now for the rest of you out there. Prepare
                   to be assimilated.

                   *The humanoid throws a big special Zap.
                   Then he disappears. Sound. Big Zap, fol-
                   lowed by virtual reality motif.*

VOICE   From now on all communication will be
                   heard in the language of the listener.

MARGOT   Dad!

JACQUES   Are you all right?

DAN   Peggy!

PEGGY   Where are we?

JACQUES   This can't be real.

VOICE   It's better than real. It's—

Sound. Virtual reality motif.

VOICE —Virtual reality!

> *JACQUES and MARGOT appear upstage right. PEGGY and DAN appear upstage left. They could now be dressed "hard drive" style.*

PEGGY *(to DAN)* Where did you get that outfit?

MARGOT *(indicating JACQUES' outfit)* Dad, you seem younger?

PEGGY And thinner?

VOICE Cholesterol has been eliminated in cyberspace.

ALL We're in Cyberspace!

> *JACQUES pulls MARGOT toward offstage right. DAN pulls PEGGY toward offstage left. They meet a force field and bounce back.*

VOICE You are inside my hard drive.

JACQUES Ridiculous!

> *During the next lines they mime invisible walls starting at opposite corners.*

DAN There's got to be a way out.

> *As they reach the down stage "wall", PEGGY notices JACQUES and MARGOT.*

PEGGY Hey...

> *The two pairs stare at each other.*

MARGOT Are you guys trapped too?

PEGGY 'Fraid so.

**JACQUES
& DAN**   You mean... we're in the same boat?

*The dads extend their hands and introduce
themselves in unison.*

DAN   Dan Martin—

JACQUES   *(French pronunciation)* Jacques Martin—

*All French names, whether of places or people,
should be pronounced in French.*

DAN   Martin?

JACQUES   Martin?

**PEGGY &
MARGOT**   This is weird.

JACQUES   Your French is pretty good for a Martin.

DAN   I don't speak French.

JACQUES   You are speaking it.

DAN   My French? No way.

PEGGY   Dad, it's like "Star Trek."

MARGOT   *(recognising a kindred spirit in PEGGY)* Yeah!
Like aliens speak Klingon,

PEGGY   *(delighted)* Or Bajoran...

MARGOT   But people from earth always understand
them.

DAN   English changes to French?

JACQUES   You mean, French becomes English?

DAN   *(light dawning)* Aha!

JACQUES	I know what this is!
MARGOT	It's a universal translator.
JACQUES	It's an Anglophone plot!
DAN	It's a Francophone plot!

> *Both dads go for each other's throats. A brief stage fight.*

PEGGY	Dad!
MARGOT	No!
PEGGY	Stop!

> *Sound. Zap. The dads are dragged behind the screen again.*

PEGGY & MARGOT	No, stop. Wait!
VOICE	I must analyse why they were fighting.
PEGGY	What's to analyse? Dad's a typical anglophone paranoid.
MARGOT	*(at the same time)* My Dad's a typical francophone paranoid.
MARGOT & PEGGY	My dad sees absolutely everything as plot.
MARGOT	Like—
PEGGY	Our cereal boxes.
MARGOT & PEGGY	Even global warming.
PEGGY	It's what we call a knee-jerk reaction.

The dads' legs appear. Dads chant "French bad/English good" and "English good/French bad" while performing knee jerks.

VOICE   Where can I find more of these jerking knees?

PEGGY   Oh, we've got plenty of them in Canada.

Sound. Accessing.

MARGOT & PEGGY   Canada.[1]

PEGGY   "A collection of huts".

MARGOT   "The land God gave to Cain",

PEGGY   "The best country in the world to live in."

MARGOT   "Not a real country."

MARGOT & PEGGY   A country that works in practice, but not in theory.

VOICE   All of Canada must be assimilated.

PEGGY   *(groaning)* Been there.

MARGOT   Done that.

DAN now appears as a NATIVE, with an oversize T-shirt that identifies him as such.

NATIVE   *(displaying it)* Bought the T-shirt.

PEGGY   *(to the NATIVE)* Where did you come from?

NATIVE   The H files.

MARGOT   You mean X files?

NATIVE H—as in history.

PEGGY But history was THEN.

MARGOT This is NOW! Please, just send us our dads back?

VOICE I have sent them back—to what you call THEN.

MARGOT Why?

VOICE In order to process the knee-jerks in NOW.

> *The NATIVE might do the cut-out paper doll trick.*

NATIVE If we seek ourselves, we must first seek our ancestors.

VOICE You have two parents, and they each had two parents, so you have four grandparents, and you have eight great-grandparents and sixteen—

PEGGY Okay, okay.

MARGOT We get the picture.

VOICE You inherited something from each of those individuals.

PEGGY &
MARGOT *(disgusted)* My curly hair.

NATIVE My black hair.

VOICE You also inherited—

> *Sound. Virtual reality motif. The actors could speak the next words in automaton-like voices.*

NATIVE   Traditions,

MARGOT   Loyalties,

PEGGY   Prejudice,

MARGOT   Power,

NATIVE   Or the lack of it.

PEGGY   Guilt.

NATIVE   Frustration.

MARGOT   Rage!

VOICE   All have been assimilated into you.

PEGGY &
MARGOT   Not in me! No way!

VOICE   Assimilation is inevitable.

PEGGY   What gives you the right?

> *JACQUES arrives in a new land as a 16th century sailor. He will be identified as CARTIER, but there's no need to specifically identify him.*

PEGGY
& DAN   *(singing)* Jacques was every inch a sailor...

NATIVE   *(to MARGOT)* What gave your dad the right?

> *JACQUES sees the NATIVE and immediately ropes him or "hammerlocks" him.[2]*

MARGOT   That's not my dad.

NATIVE   It's your Dad to the Nth squared.

JACQUES   I'm in here, Margot, along with a lot of
           other guys.

VOICE   Many generations are inhabiting one body.

NATIVE   Yeah. *(from the floor)* Your basic "white
           man who steals other people's countries"
           body.

MARGOT   Well, Dad to the Nth squared, *(freeing the
           Native from the sailor's rope)* that was a rot-
           ten way to start a relationship.

PEGGY   Yeah, I mean... it wasn't gobbledygook.

CARTIER   I don't understand.

PEGGY   Strong-arming the Natives was dookeldy-
           gob.

CARTIER   Gobbledygook? Dookeldygob?

MARGOT   Has the translator stopped working?

VOICE   I cannot translate what you mean by
           "right" and "wrong" to an historic charac-
           ter.

PEGGY   Why not?

VOICE   Morality and Ethics are time sensitive.
           How you judge actions in NOW time
           makes no sense to people from THEN time.

NATIVE   *(pointing to JACQUES)* But he made a
           choice, didn't he?

CARTIER   Not really. I mean... one moment I was sail-
           ing off the coast of France, and the next
           minute this great big tide of circumstance
           rose up, and—

           Sound. Ocean waves.

MARGOT   Tide of circumstance?

CARTIER   When you look at history, Margot, there are
           huge events which pick people up and
           carry them along, just like a wave would.
           And if you're caught in a wave, you go
           with the flow. The wave I was on... well, it
           kinda started with one new idea.

               *He distributes insignia or whatever for a SCI-
               ENTIST (PEGGY).*

SCIENTIST The sun doesn't circle the earth!

CARTIER   You're kidding!

SCIENTIST The sun stands still. We're the ones that
           move.

CARTIER   But... if the earth is not the centre of the
           universe... that calls everything I was
           taught into question.

               *The head of AUTHORITY pops up over the
               screen. His costume should be divided as to
               colour, half red and half blue so he can be
               French or English in profile as circumstance
               dictates.*

AUTH   It's not your place to question anything.

CARTIER   Who are you?

AUTH   *(making a noose out of the electrical cord)* I am
           Authority, and I hate questions.

SCIENTIST I wonder... what if the world were round?

AUTH   Heretic! Off with his head!

               *AUTHORITY loops the noose around his
               neck.*

SCIENTIST Wait a minute! Authority, your lordship, suppose you could make money out of this particular question?

AUTH Money?

SCIENTIST The riches of the Orient!

AUTH *(letting go of the rope)* I love money.

SCIENTIST We'd get there faster by sailing west.

AUTH Money gives me more control.

CABOT *(PEGGY)* I, John Cabot, claim this new world for England.[3]

CARTIER *(JACQUES)* I, Jacques Cartier, claim this new world for France.

NATIVE *(tapping him on the shoulder)* Exactly how do you define claim?[4]

CARTIER Cut! You didn't ask that THEN, so you can't ask it NOW.

NATIVE I tried to ask it THEN.

CARTIER Even the universal translator can't interpret retroactively. So... listen, buddy, wanta trade that pelt for this nice knife?

NATIVE Wow... sharp! What'll you give me for this beat-up old beaver?

A European beaver hat appears.

JACQUES Wow! Sharp!

MARGOT & PEGGY *(as Europeans)* Wow. Sharp! I want a beaver hat! Gotta have a beaver hat.

VOICE	Meanwhile, in a lower socio-economic bracket.
PEGGY	Boiled beans and cabbage for dinner again!
MARGOT	No, dear. Try the latest staple of choice.
PEGGY	Fishsticks!
MARGOT	Salt fishsticks.

> *JACQUES changes his logo from SAILOR to FRENCH SETTLER. PEGGY dons an ENGLISH SETTLER indicator. In the script they are simply designated FRENCH and ENGLISH.*

AUTH	Clearly, there is cash in New World fur and fish. The name of the game is Monopoly.

> *MARGOT produces an oversize dice and oversize Chance cards, and places them strategically.*

FRENCH	*(miming digging in hard ground and singing to the tune of "Sixteen Tons")* You till the land in Europe and what do you get...
AUTH	*(indicating or revealing map)* And this is the board.
ENGLISH	*(also digging)* Another day older and deeper in debt.
AUTH	Hey, you... yeah, you. *(rolling dice)* How would you like a chance at a better life?

> *Sound. Waves.*

ENGLISH	I feel a great wave of circumstance raising me up... *(miming being propelled across stage)* Ohhhhh...

FRENCH   *(miming being propelled across stage)*
             Ohhhhh...

FRENCH &
ENGLISH   Where the *(computer beeps)* am I now?

             MARGOT places Port Royal in blue and
             Cupids⁵ in red on the map.

AUTH   First French colony, first English colony.

JACQUES   *(breaking character)* Computer, don't we
             need another player?

DAN   Yeah, English authority and French author-
             ity... shouldn't they be different?

VOICE   They both coveted wealth and power. They
             performed the same actions to achieve their
             goals. French and English are irrelevant.

JACQUES   I knew it!

DAN   This isn't virtual reality! It is—

JACQUES   It is—

DAN   *(putting a strangle hold on JACQUES)* ...a
             Francophone plot!

JACQUES   *(putting a strangle hold on DAN)* ...an
             Anglophone plot!

             PEGGY and MARGOT separate DAN and
             JACQUES.

MARGOT   Okay, okay. Dad, suppose he turns his blue
             side when he's French.

PEGGY   And a red one when he's English?

AUTH   Roll'em.

        MARGOT rolls dice.

AUTHORITY   Pick up a card.

MARGOT   *(she turns one over)* War.

FRENCH   Hey, Anglo! *(grabbing a gun)* We don't mind you fishing off The Rock over there, but the rest of the continent isn't big enough for both of us!

ENGLISH   *(grabbing a gun)* We'll see about that!

JACQUES   *(breaking character)* Cut!

PEGGY   What's wrong now?

JACQUES   If the translator can't be retroactive, she and I can't understand each other.

MARGOT   Oh! I learned the answer to that in school. In THEN time French was the language of diplomacy.

JACQUES   Oh, in that case... *(he shoots)* Bang!

ENGLISH   *(returning fire)* Bang!

MARGOT   I said diplomacy, Dad.

ENGLISH   It's not enough to be able to talk.

FRENCH   You gotta want to.

VOICE   In THEN time fighting was a respected occupation.

MARGOT   That's disgusting.

FRENCH   Margot, you understand how we didn't know about the Americas before we discovered them...?

NATIVE   Invaded.

MARGOT   Encountered.

FRENCH   There were a lot of ideas we hadn't encountered either—for instance, nobody, but
nobody, had ever had the thought that war
was wrong, and *(to the NATIVE)* that
includes you.

> *FRENCH places a big blue dot on the map.*[6]

NATIVE   *(to French)* Hold it. A trading post on the
coast is one thing, but that is my square
and you owe me big time.

FRENCH   All right, let's discuss this. I wonder... by
any chance... do you folks have enemies?[7]

> *MARGOT dons a NATIVE 2 logo.*

NATIVE   Well, we're not very fond of that nation
there.

FRENCH   That "nation" there?

NATIVE   You think you're the only one with a rival
nation?

FRENCH   *(shooting)* Bang. *(the NATIVE collapses)*
The enemy of my friend is my enemy.
(passing the gun) So, I get to found Quebec
City?

> *The ENGLISH SETTLER helps the fallen
> NATIVE up and gives him a gun.*

ENGLISH   The enemy of my enemy is my friend.

**FRENCH &
ENGLISH**   *(producing a flask of rum each for the
NATIVES)* Let's drink to becoming allies.

NATIVES   All right!

VOICE   Nobody in THEN time had heard of the Prime Directive.

**FRENCH &
ENGLISH**   Prime Directive?

VOICE   Interfering in other cultures is a no no.

**FRENCH &
ENGLISH**   Only in outer space.

NATIVES   Pity.

> *NATIVE and FRENCH shake hands.*

FRENCH   My name is Abraham Martin, by the way.

> *PEGGY and MARGOT drop out of character.*

**MARGOT
& PEGGY**   My grandfather's name was Abraham Martin![8]

FRENCH   *(putting his arms around both girls)* I'm your granddad—well, your granddad's grand-dad's granddad.

**PEGGY &
MARGOT**   *(to each other)* Then we're—cousins?

VOICE   Relatively speaking.

MARGOT   Do you like Kevin Parent?

PEGGY   *(indicating no)* How about Corey Hart?

**MARGOT
& PEGGY**   Leonardo Di Caprio! Like Dreamy! Wanta go to a movie?

FRENCH	Girls, right now... right THEN, I mean, those plains in Quebec City are being named after our family.
MARGOT & PEGGY	Big deal.
FRENCH	Oh, they will be, believe me.
NATIVE	In the meantime, my name is Wendat, but you will call me Huron,[9] which is, relatively speaking, an insult.
FRENCH	Without the translator you don't know that.
ENGLISH	I'll call you Iroquois, and *(to the audience)* you'll probably call me the bad guy, but— like the computer said, it's relative.

All face the audience.

ALL	The British and French fight so many wars throughout this story that we're not going to bother with a lot of dates, okay?
AUTH	*(rolling dice)* Come on my babies. Come on to mama.
ENGLISH	WE didn't just make war. We started New England.

AUTHORITY keeps rolling dice. ENGLISH and FRENCH place their possessions on the map.

FRENCH	WE built forts along the whole length of the St. Lawrence. We expanded along the rivers that flowed down—
OTHERS	*(singing the last line of the "Battle of New Orleans")* Down the Mississippi to the Gulf of Mexico.

FRENCH   Where did you get that line?

MARGOT   I don't know...

PEGGY   From the computer, I guess.

ENGLISH   Well, forts can be captured! *(shooting)* Bang!

FRENCH   And— *(shooting)* Bang! Bang!—recaptured!

> *Show Detroit, Quebec, Louisbourg Newfoundland etc. going back and forth.*

ENGLISH   But your king gave this one back to our king.

FRENCH   But your king gave Quebec back to us.

> *Quebec goes blue again. Newfoundland goes red again.*

FRENCH & ENGLISH   What you win in the forests, you lose in the treaties.

MARGOT   Hit the Escape key! I mean History is boring, but the history of warring and exploring is really boring.

VOICE   It is not.

MARGOT   And as for treaties—like click on Exit fast.

PEGGY   My cousin is right. Wasn't there any romance?

> *Sound. Accessing.*

VOICE   Once upon a time on a cold winter night...

> *PEGGY and JACQUES go off as DAN and
> MARGOT take on the roles of teenage ETI-
> ENNE BRÛLÉ type and young NATIVE
> GIRL. A mime underscored by a romantic
> French folksong. The NATIVE GIRL and
> ETIENNE BRÛLÉ see each other, approach
> shyly, attempt to communicate, and commu-
> nicate falling in love. When they are in an
> embrace, JACQUES becomes SAMUEL de
> CHAMPLAIN. The couple jumps apart.*

FRENCH No, no... it's okay.

ETIENNE May I introduce Samuel de Champlain?

GIRL *(disinterested)* Hi. *(she returns to lovemaking)*

FRENCH You youngsters have given me a vision of a
new nation... half French, half native... you
could create a true north culture that is
strong and free... and *(as they kiss)* maybe
fun.

AUTH Make a new plan, Sam! The tide of history
has brought the Ancien Régime to Nouvelle
France.

ALL The what?

AUTH The Ancien Régime. *(pointing up)* God,
(lowering his hand at each class) the Pope, the
king, the aristocrats who will own all this
land, and the Peasants.

ETIENNE Habitants, pul-eeze.

AUTH Whatever. You do the work and pay the
aristocrats rent.

ETIENNE I'd rather paddle my own canoe.

AUTH   (*grabbing him by the ear*) I am also your Holy Mother Church, my son, and I am going to spank you so hard you won't be able to sit in a canoe for the rest of the seventeenth century.

ETIENNE   (*putting his arm around the girl*) Then I guess she and I will have to head west.

GIRL   (*to AUTHORITY*) We're going to create the half-French, half-Native, Métis nation without you.

AUTH   You can't outrun the wave of history in a birch bark canoe.

ETIENNE   (*derisive*) Even your wave can't reach as far as Manitoba.

> The NATIVE GIRL and ETIENNE BRÛLÉ exit, arms around each other. SAM waves good-bye, sadly.

FRENCH   (*to AUTHORITY*) If only you'd let me, I could build a Canada that includes (*gesturing to where the couple exited*) them, but does not include the greed and brutality of the old World.

AUTH   New World, Old World, fiddlesticks. I am absolute, and I rule the WHOLE world absolutely.

> PEGGY enters as ENGLISH, and DAN reverts to the NATIVE.

ENGLISH   Except—

AUTH   There are no exceptions.

ENGLISH   EXCEPT between the dis— *(catching her-self)* encountering of North America and the settlement of New England, Old England had become Protestant.

          JACQUES and MARGOT sing "The Huron Carol" underneath the next section.

AUTH   Nouvelle France will be Catholic. *(to the NATIVE)* We're bringing priests to convert you.

NATIVE   *(to the audience)* That's another word for assimilate.

AUTH   *(rolling dice)* When you see how superior our customs are, you won't mind a bit.

NATIVE   In your dreams, maybe. You think we don't mind those European diseases that are wiping us out?

AUTH   Oops.

          The NATIVE takes the dice and rolls them.

NATIVE   *(passing him a card)* There's one custom you don't need to teach us.

AUTH   *(reading)* French-Iroquois wars.

ALL   Bang! Bang!

          The NATIVE mimes burning FRENCH at a stake. Perhaps he lights a match, or flicks his lighter. FRENCH crosses himself.

NATIVE   Assimilation is not inevitable.

AUTH   Then it's going to be a numbers game and
            we're going to get the numbers. *(to the
            FRENCH SETTLER)* You! Get down from
            there. I order you to start having babies,
            lots and lots of babies.

FRENCH   Without women?

AUTH   Oh... okay, give me a minute. *(MARGOT
            enters as a poor, French orphan FILLE)* You
            there...

FILLE   Me?

AUTH   The girl with no family, no money, and no
            future except the street.

FILLE   That's me.

AUTH   My darling daughter... I am your Sun King
            of France and I'm going to make you an
            offer you can't refuse.

            Sound. Ocean waves.

FILLE   Ohhhhh. It feels like a great big wave... [10]
            the Sun King is sending me to marry a
            Canadian. Ooohhh... there are seven hun-
            dred and seventy-four other girls surfing
            along! No, oh, no! They're all prettier than
            me.

            *FILLE mimes being carried by a wave and
            tossed into the arms of FRENCH.*

FRENCH   And they snagged the hunks. So you're
            stuck with me.

FILLE   Are you a steady worker? Do you have a
            nice farm?

FRENCH   I'm a Coureur du Bois, baby, a Voyageur.

FILLE	At least I suppose you'll be kind?
FRENCH	*(forcing her to her knees)* Scrub the floor, cook up a storm, and I might be. As long as you keep me... real happy. *(he breaks character)* Hey, why is this guy such a jerk?
DAN	Yeah, even Anglophones agree that the Voyageurs were great types.
PEGGY	This is the Fille du Roi's point of view.
JACQUES	But the Voyageurs opened the country,
DAN	Wore colourful clothes and sang cute songs.

JACQUES and DAN break into one.

MARGOT	*(shouting over them)* And what did the women do?
JACQUES	The Filles du Roi were a footnote in history.
PEGGY	*(looking at MARGOT)* Because men like our dads—
MARGOT	*(looking at PEGGY)* —wrote the history books.
MARGOT	*(to PEGGY)* Are you thinking what I'm thinking?
PEGGY	Serve him right.

The girls dress JACQUES as the FILLE.

MARGOT	*(to JACQUES)* My, Fille du Roi, you sure got old...
PEGGY	And ugly.
JACQUES	Seventeen years in the wilderness with that ne'er-do-well would age anybody.

NATIVE   *(shooting)* Bang!

MARGOT   Oops. Papa's been wasted.

FILLE   I'm left with thirteen sous in my pocket and eight mouths to feed. Please, computer, beam me back to Paris.

MARGOT   *(becoming a seventeenth-century teenager)*
Mama to the Nth squared, listen!

FILLE   My little girl! You look just like me when I was young.

MARGOT   Mama, Papa was carrying a bundle of furs.

FILLE   Oh! I'll sell them to the merchants in Montreal.

> *FILLE takes the bundle of furs and crosses the stage.*

AUTH   I'll collect twenty-five percent of those.

> *The FILLE begins to pay. MARGOT stops her.*

MARGOT   You've got to be kidding!

FILLE   We are on a New France monopoly square.

MARGOT   But a twenty-five percent tax is worse than the GST.

AUTH   If you don't pay, you go to jail.

MARGOT   Oh, yeah! I'm fed up, and I'm not going to take it anymore.

FILLE   *(feeling a wave rise beneath her feet)*
Ohhhhh... stop! You're making a wave.

AUTH   Good little girls don't make waves.

FILLE   *(being propelled across the stage)* Ohhhhh...
           Margot...

AUTH   Where is she gone?

MARGOT   To Plattsburg.[11] To sell her furs at a decent
           price.

AUTH   That's smuggling!

MARGOT   That's reverse cross-border shopping.

           *The FILLE enters with PEGGY as a NATIVE
           on a rope.*

FILLE   Look, dear. I bought her from a woman in
           New York. *(she jerks the rope and the
           NATIVE stumbles forward)*[12] Slaves are all
           the rage in the English colonies.

           *FILLE busies herself with something. MAR-
           GOT goes to the NATIVE and unties her.*

MARGOT   What's your name?

VOICE   She cannot answer you. She has no voice
           in THEN anymore.

MARGOT   She still has legs. Quick, run!

FILLE   There's nowhere for her to run. Her tribe's
           been wiped out.

MARGOT   But Mama...

FILLE   It was a war, dear.

MARGOT   Mama, that's dookledygob.

FILLE   Her people lost.

MARGOT   But slavery is dookledygob.

FILLE   I don't understand, dear. But won't it be wonderful—

MARGOT   *(breaking character)* Dad!

FILLE   —to have someone else to scrub our floors?

MARGOT   Dad! Snap out of it!

FILLE   But you can't stop history just because you don't like it, dear. *(changing DAN into the Coureur De Bois PIERRE outfit)* And look, I've found you a rich boyfriend.

MARGOT   Another stupid voyageur.

PIERRE   *(bowing)[13]* Pierre Radisson, at your service.

FILLE   This guy beat Authority at Monopoly.

AUTH   He cheated.

PIERRE   I started the Hudson's Bay Company.

        PIERRE makes the map around Hudson's Bay red.

MARGOT   Smooth move.

AUTH   For the English! You are a traitor to France.

MARGOT   Yeah, well... Canada is my country.

AUTH   What is this Canada? There is no Canada yet. New France is blue and it extends all the way from here...

        The actors update the map. A huge section of the map is blue.

MARGOT   Manitoba was French?

AUTH   ...to—

ALL   (*singing*) "Down the Mississippi to the Gulf of Mexico."

AUTH   No. That's still the wrong cue.

PEGGY   It must be some glitch in the computer.

AUTH   Pierre Radisson spoiled that pretty blue with that ugly red blob.

DAN   There was bound to be an outbreak of red pretty soon.

             PEGGY, DAN, JACQUES and MARGOT mime a Monopoly game. Rolling dice, moving markers, picking cards. They adjust the map as they play.

MARGOT   English immigration to New England increases ten-fold as we move into the 18th century.

PEGGY   English settlers overflow into the North, into the Maritimes. The city of Halifax becomes the centre of British authority.[14]

             She adds red to the map.

JACQUES   You can't do that!

MARGOT   That's Acadie!

PEGGY   Nova Scotia swallows Acadia whole.

MARGOT   What will happen to the French population?

PEGGY   Their fate will be decided by— (*picking a card and passing it to MARGOT*)

MARGOT   (*taking the card*) The Seven Years War.[15]

JACQUES   That was a really big Bang Bang.

MARGOT	And it made a really big wave.
	Sound. Ocean waves. JACQUES and MARGOT are caught by the wave.
JACQUES & MARGOT	Au secours!
AUTH	*(pointing to JACQUES and MARGOT)* Did I hear a foreign accent?
JACQUES	We have nothing to do with the fighting.
MARGOT	*(appealing to DAN who becomes NEW ENGLANDER)* Please, please, this is our home.
AUTH	You might stab us in the back!
NEW ENG	Listen, Authority, they've been my neighbours for a while, eh?
AUTH	It's time for ethnic cleansing. *(NEW ENGLANDER hesitates)* If I expel them, you can annex their land.[16]
	PEGGY grabs MARGOT and JACQUES and pushes them in the opposite directions.
NEW ENG	Gotta go with the flow.
ACADIAN	Oh, my country...
NEW ENG	I mean, I was living in the Age of Enlightenment.
ACADIAN	What have I done that you should drive me away...
NEW ENG	And enlightenment meant progress— Protestant, commercial progress.
FRENCH	Oh, my country...

NEW ENG   Maybe in NOW time you'd understand it better if I said "market forces" or "business is business?"

ACADIAN   Why was I herded onto a crowded ship?

NEW ENG   I mean, watch your TV news. Market forces count a lot more than individual rights...

ACADIAN   I become a cast-away in a foreign town...

NEW ENG   Or even the rights of nation states.

ACADIAN   Never again to lay eyes on the faces of my friends.

NEW ENG   Maybe if we'd been in B.C. in the nineteen-forties, the government would have just shipped them up to the mountains.

ACADIAN   I labour without understanding, among those who know nothing of mine, or of me.

NEW ENG   If it were Africa NOW, some peace-keeping force might establish a refugee camp. But it was THEN, eh?

ACADIAN   Oh, my country.

ACADIAN exits.

NEW ENG   And it WAS war, and it was touch and go for the next five years... until destiny sent a British fleet eighty miles long up the St. Lawrence.

DAN enters as a NEWFOUNDLANDER.

NEWF   It weren't just the English regulars, b'y.
           Some Newfs were there too. *(to the audi-
           ence)* Oh, I don't expect you to know that.
           We'um never makes much news on the
           mainland. The t'ing was, ever since the six-
           teen hundreds, the French'd come down off
           and on and burn St. John's. Once they cap-
           tured the whole of Newfoundland, except
           for a tiny island in Conception Bay. One of
           those times I lost my wife and child, eh? I
           don't recollect how much longer after they
           were kilt that the French went away and
           the British came back, and I tried to go on
           fishing like always. But then I got wind
           there was another fight brewing, up away
           on the French doorstep. So me and the b'ys
           took the notion that we might put some of
           that goose sauce back on the gander.
           (pause)[17] The General had the name of
           Wolfe, and wolf weren't a bad name for
           him. It were enough to turn your stomach
           the way he had us burning out the French
           farmers all the way up river. But Quebec
           City, well, our guns pounded her to
           smithereens all summer... but she wouldn't
           fall. And we wakes up one morning and
           there's a skim of ice on the river, and ifen
           we stayed much longer we would been
           trapped. So Wolfe, he calls us together...
           and he sez, "Lads, how would you fancy a
           spot of rock climbing?

MARGOT   *(whispering a warning)* Montcalm?

NEWF   The only thing about it, sez Wolfe, if you
           feel yourself falling, you can't cry out.
           'Cause that'd give the game away.

MARGOT   *(more urgently)* Montcalm!

NEWF   Well, it were some dark, and it were some
             slippery, and I don't know how many times
             there'd be a scrape of stones and the
             whoosh of a body pitchin' past... there must
             a been a thump when they landed, but,
             b'ys, I never heard a single scream that
             night.

MARGOT   Montcalm, wake up!

NEWF   I were almost at the top when I felt myself
             go. I clamped my jaw shut and keep her
             shut all the way down the drop. Ifen I'd
             yelled, you see, all the b'ys would be as
             dead as me.

MARGOT   For the love of God, Montcalm, wake up!

             PEGGY as MILITARY HISTORIAN enters.
             The other actors play this out with puppets or
             toys or whatever.

MIL HIST Montcalm woke up to find the British on
             the Plains of Abraham. He formed his
             army into the classic French fighting forma-
             tion—the renowned blue column, that is, a
             dense mass of soldiers marching shoulder
             to shoulder, drummer boys hidden in the
             middle, drumming steadily, implacably,
             relentlessly toward the enemy.

             Sound. Amplified marching feet and drums.

MIL HIST Wolfe spread out his forces only two sol-
             diers deep; a thin red line—because the
             problem with a column is that only the sol-
             diers in the front line can fire. The ones in
             back would shoot their comrades if they
             did. And, of course, the guns in THEN
             time could fire only once.

MARGOT   Bang!

MIL HIST   Only the front rank of English can fire too, but because they are spread out and not moving, their bang can inflict more damage.

DAN   Bang!

MIL HIST   After that first volley, the blue column must reload as they march. But the front rank of the English drop to their knees, and at that instant, the second rank fires over their heads.

DAN   Bang!

MIL HIST   By the time they've fired, the front rank is ready to fire again.

DAN   *(alternating high and low)* Bang. Bang. Bang. Bang.

    Silence.

MIL HIST   Inside fifteen minutes, the battle on the Plains of Abraham Martin, and, to all intents and purposes, Canada, is won by the English.

DAN   *(breaking character)* Okay, that's it. Game over.

JACQUES   I still have shots left.

MARGOT   What is captured can be recaptured.

VOICE   I'll give them one more chance.

    JACQUES addresses the audience.

JACQUES   All winter every inhabitant of Nouvelle France prayed—

MARGOT   And prayed—

JACQUES   And prayed—

MARGOT   That when the ice on the river melted...

JACQUES   When ships can reach us again...

MARGOT &
JACQUES   The French Navy will come and set us free!

DAN   But the first ships up the river that spring were British.

PEGGY   By the end of summer, Montreal surrendered.[18]

DAN   Prepare to be assimilated.

JACQUES   No, no, wait! When the war ends in Europe there'll be a treaty.

>   *PEGGY dons glove puppets of Louis XV and VOLTAIRE.*

MARGOT   Our king always makes your king give stuff back.

VOLTAIRE   *(pointing to the board)* We can negotiate to retain some of our squares, Majesty, but not all of them. *(picking a card)* You must choose between these exquisite sandy beaches... *(he reveals Club Med-type tourist ad for Martinique)* Or a few acres of snow.[19]

>   *Sound. A very brief parody of "Hands Up," the Club Med theme. The actors update the map. North America is 99 percent red. Sound. A ship's horn.*

AUTH   All aboard the *S.S. Martinque*...

MARGOT &
JACQUES   Hey, wait for us!

AUTH	Governing class only, I'm afraid. Bye, bye, habitants.
DAN	We won. You lost.
JACQUES	We did not lose.
AUTH	Bye, bye.
JACQUES	We were abandoned.
DAN	Anyway you slice it, Canada became English and you—
JACQUES	Don't you dare—
DAN	You have to face it—
JACQUES	DON'T—
DAN	The French in Canada—
JACQUES	YOU—
DAN	—are a conquered people.
JACQUES	DARE!

JACQUES and DAN go for each other's throats again, but MARGOT and PEGGY pull them apart. Each speaks to her father, beginning in unison.

PEGGY & MARGOT	Dad, I don't mean to hurt your feelings or anything, but...
PEGGY	You are being, like... totally insensitive... and kinda of—grossly ignorant?
MARGOT	And Dad, for me, personally, I will not accept that my future has anything to do with "bang" versus "bang bang."

JACQUES   Listen, Anglo, all I want is for you and your
             kind to get off my back.

DAN   You want, you want, you want! The British
             should never have let you keep your lan-
             guage and your laws.

VOICE   You mean the Conquerors did not assimi-
             late the Conquered?

             DAN dons the ENGLISH military hat.

ENGLISH   Force isn't necessary. When the French see
             how superior our customs are, they'll beg
             to be assimilated.

JACQUES   *(picking up a gun)* In your dreams, maybe.

AUTH   *(to JACQUES)* My son, my son... *(taking the
             gun from him)* Good little boys don't play
             with guns.

JACQUES   How can you say that! You're Canadian,
             aren't you?

AUTH   I'm Canadian authority. The English and I
             understand each other.

JACQUES   Because French was the language of diplo-
             macy?

AUTH   French, smench. I mean, me... authority.

MARGOT   I think he's talking about Divine Order
             again—as in God, *(lowering her hand a little)*
             the Pope...

ENGLISH   The king...

JACQUES   Not the English king?

AUTH   Anybody's king is friend of authority.

ENGLISH   Right. So even after our conquest...

AUTH   Our French church can hold fast to The Ancien Regime.

ENGLISH   We call it The Great Chain of Being.

AUTH   Whatever. The important thing is...

ENGLISH & AUTH   We are at the top, and you're at the bottom.

YANKEE   *(off)* Bang!

ENGLISH   What's that?

> *PEGGY enters singing "Yankee Doodle."*
> *AUTHORITY covers JACQUES' ears.*

MARGOT   It sounded like another Bang.

YANKEE   A bang? That was the "shot heard round the world!"

ENGLISH   *(picking a card)* The American Revolution.

YANKEE   We the people want a word with him. *(indicating Jacques)*

ENGLISH   *(as if it were a new word)* Peep... al?

AUTH   Peep-al?

YANKEE   As in "We the people" who are all created equal?

ENGLISH & AUTH   *(another new word)* Eeek-well?

YANKEE   *(to JACQUES)* We—you and I... ordinary people. These guys.... him and him... the enemies of the people!

AUTH   *(still covering JACQUES' ears)* He can't hear a word you're saying.

YANKEE   *(singing to "Battle of New Orleans")* We fired our guns and the British started running/

ENGLISH   So the map's not red like it was a while ago/

YANKEE   We invited the Quebecers—

MARGOT   —But they were not forthcoming

ALL   Down the Mississippi to the Gulf of Mexico.

MARGOT   Was that the right cue?

> *YANKEE adjusts the map, then exits.*

ENGLISH   Yeah.

MARGOT   Finally.

ENGLISH   The Yankees chased the British right out of what became the United States. *(to FRENCH AUTHORITY)* But if you French had joined them, we would have lost the whole continent. Thank you, thank you, thank you.

> *Music. "La Marseillaise."*

JACQUES   What's that?

ENGLISH   *(holding JACQUES firmly)* It's the French Revolution passing you by.

AUTH   *(to the ENGLISH)* He might have chopped off my head. Thank you, thank you.

**ENGLISH
& AUTH**   The enemy of my enemy is my friend.
             We're still at the top!

ENGLISH exits to become ABRAHAM.

JACQUES   And I'm still at the bottom.

AUTH   Just cultivate your garden. Raise a daugh-
               ter named Marguerite and a son named
               Abraham Martin the third.

DAN enters as ABRAHAM.

ABRAHAM   That's me. Dad, I want to get married.

*PEGGY enters as ENGLISH MARGARET, a
young UEL.*

JACQUES   She looks English.

ABRAHAM   She's a United Empire Loyalist.[20]

E. MARG   My parents came to Canada after the revo-
               lution back in the States.

*MARGOT enters as FRENCH MAR-
GUERITE.*

MARGOT   Along with 40,000 others.

ABRAHAM   Marguerite, I want you to meet Margaret.
               *(MARGUERITE turns her back to MAR-
               GARET)*

F. MARG   Her people have taken all the jobs and most
               of the good land.

E. MARG   That's not my fault.

F. MARG   We've become so poor, I have to scrub
               floors for people like you.

JACQUES   *(to ABRAHAM)* I suppose we'll try to love her, if she learns French and joins the Church.

ABRAHAM   Actually, papa...

E. MARG   Abe and I are about to start the English speaking, Protestant branch of the Martin family.

F. MARG   You've stolen the good life I once had... and now you're stealing my brother!

JACQUES   Marguerite, you have no such brother. I have no such son.

     FRENCH MARGUERITE writes or pins Long Live French or some such on the board.

PEGGY   But Margot, this is how we get to be related.

F. MARG   You English were awful to us! I hate you! I don't want to be related to you.

PEGGY   Maybe not in THEN time, but—

MARGOT   Not then... and not in NOW time either!

     JACQUES adds an anti-English slogan and exits. PEGGY resumes ENGLISH MARGARET.

E. MARG   Let's go west. We'll create a province of our own.

E. MARG &
ABRAHAM   Give us a place to stand and a place to grow/ and we will build Ontari—

AUTH   —Upper Canada. *(ENGLISH MARGARET and ABRAHAM create Upper Canada and Lower Canada on the map)* And I, as a series of British Governors, am in absolute control of both Upper and Lower for the next fifty odd years.

                Sound. Gentle ocean waves.

E. MARG   Abraham, when British Authority says that word...

ABRAHAM   Control?

E. MARG   I feel... I don't know, suddenly seasick?

AUTH   What are all these little waves splashing all around my feet?

ABRAHAM   They're ideas. Ideas about *(miming dipping his toe in or testing water with his hand)* justice and fairness and oh... *(whispering)* Democracy.

E. MARG   Democracy... would I like democracy?

AUTH   Not a bit. *(PEGGY and ABRAHAM look uncertain)* No, guys, trust me. Canadians don't need American ideas. Canadians fought a war against Americans in 1812. Don't you remember? You chased them...

ABRAHAM
& E. MARG   Down the Mississippi to—

AUTH   No! To Washington D.C. where you...

E. MARG   Wait! *(testing the water)* War is... dookledy-gob. *(gleefully)* Okay, tell them what we did.

AUTH   You burned the White House.

E. MARG   Yea Canada!

ABRAHAM   One for us!

Sound. Ocean waves become louder.

E. MARG   But we've come to 1830 and—

ABRAHAM   Watch out!

E. MARG   The waves of ideas are getting bigger!

ABRAHAM   *(splashing in one)* Human rights!

E. MARG   Oh... slavery is... wrong.

ABRAHAM   Yeah. It's wrong.

PEGGY   You heard wrong, not "dookledygob?"

AUTH   Slavery is outlawed throughout the British Empire... you see, I am not entirely a monster.

ABRAHAM   Then please, sir, will you let me go surfing?

AUTH   On the democracy wave? No way!

E. MARG   But the water's knee-high in Toronto.

ABRAHAM   The Upper Canadian farmers are revolting.

AUTH   I agree. They're smelly too.

ABRAHAM   No, I mean... we're taking up arms against your graft and corruption!

E. MARG   The wave has reached Quebec City!

AUTH   Get out the sandbags!

> *MARGOT piles everything she can lay her hands on against the flood, JACQUES as PAPINEAU is propelled on stage.*

PAPINEAU   The democratic flood has poured irresistibly down the slope of time—

AUTH   More sandbags!

PAPINEAU   —And, growing faster and faster—

AUTH   Build a dam!

PAPINEAU   —will topple the unavailing barriers which may be erected against it.[21]

> *PAPINEAU kicks over whatever AUTHORITY has built.*

E. MARG &
ABRAHAM   *(chanting)* Papineau, Papineau, long live Papineau and Liberty.

> *Add graffiti to all surfaces whenever possible from here on in.*

PAPINEAU   The French majority demand a voice in their government.

AUTH   Insolent, insane, ridiculous idiot!

PAPINEAU   We demand our voice in our own French language.

E. MARG   Good for you![22] The Patriots of Upper—

PAPINEAU   —and Lower Canada—

ALL   —share the same hopes and dreams for their children's future.

ABRAHAM   If we could get our act together we might defeat this tyrant. *(he picks up a gun and aims it at AUTHORITY)*

AUTH   *(standard cop show-down)* Come now, you're a farmer, not a soldier. In your heart of hearts, you don't want to be a murderer, do you? You're a Canadian, you're nice. So why don't you just hand over that gun?

> *ABRAHAM lowers his gun. AUTHORITY loops the noose around ABRAHAM's neck.*

E. MARG   *(kneeling)* He didn't kill anyone. He never fired a shot. You can't hang him!

AUTH   I can and I will.

E. MARG   Please, have mercy. *(AUTHORITY kicks her out of his way, and strangles ABE with the rope)* No, please, please, no!

> *MARGARET drags ABRAHAM's body off stage.*[23]

AUTH   *(turning to PAPINEAU)* I offer a thousand pounds to anyone who will put this same noose around Papineau's treasonous neck.

PAPINEAU   Why? The British are the only ones killing people. Canadians are the only ones who have died!

AUTH   Until a British officer named Jack Weir finds himself alone in the village of St. Denis.[24]

> *PEGGY is generic ENGLISH again.*

PAPINEAU   That was a horrible accident.

MARGOT   It was like the riots you see on television. No one planned to kill him.

PAPINEAU   One group of people are angry at another group... and they're protesting or demonstrating, and then, suddenly—

MARGOT   Hey look! There's one of THEM!

PAPINEAU   A century of rage spilled out of the villagers.

MARGOT   That rage was inflicted on one unfortunate man.

ENGLISH   Other English soldiers found his body in the river. It gave British Authority the excuse he needed.

AUTH   We no longer have to treat Papineau and his followers as citizens with honest demands.

ENGLISH   They are rebels! Criminals!

PAPINEAU   But it was an accident!

ENGLISH   Come on, fight! We want to fight!

PAPINEAU   *(exiting)* It takes two to fight and I refuse.

AUTH   There is always someone who wants to be a hero.

            MARGOT becomes CHENIER.

ENGLISH   Fight! I want a fight!

CHENIER   I shall win freedom for my people or die in the attempt.

ENGLISH   Then die! Die in the burning church at St. Eustache.[25]

            ENGLISH kills CHENIER with fire and sword.

AUTH   The rebels are buried in unhallowed
            ground. And in memory of the English
            officer, the dead French body of Jean
            Olivier Chenier is—dissected.

ENGLISH   Remember Jack Weir.

CHENIER   Remember Jean Chenier!

PEGGY   *(breaking character)* I don't remember either
            of them.

MARGOT   Me neither.

AUTH   The names of the victims weren't impor-
            tant. But they provided me with an excuse
            for wholesale slaughter. The resulting
            hatred divides French from English for gen-
            erations.

MARGOT
& PEGGY   I hate you!

            *MARGOT and PEGGY exit. The monstrous
            effigy of LORD DURHAM appears.*

DURHAM   We can't have two nations warring in the
            bosom of single state. The French in
            Canada must be assimilated.

OTHERS   *(off)* Hiss. Boo.

            *The man behind the effigy is revealed (DAN).
            He is totally charming, with lots of sex
            appeal, and has a warm, disarming smile.*

DURHAM   All right, hiss, boo, throw your tomatoes. I
            did recommend assimilation back THEN.
            Were I here NOW, I should put it the other
            way round—that the Francophones must
            assimilate the Anglophones from sea to
            shining sea.

AUTH   Sir, you're outrageous!

DURHAM   *(modestly)* I'm Durham, actually. *(to the audience)* You see, when the British Government sent me to Quebec I didn't get the chance to experience a show by Robert LePage, or a film by Denys Arcand. I never had a chance to hear Celine Dion. Back in THEN time, it never occurred to me that the Francophones could create a vibrant culture despite being surrounded by the wholesale mediocrity that the rest of North America has contrived to become. *(ENGLISH enters with JACQUES on a rope)* I say, what do you think you're doing?

ENGLISH   He's a rebel, sentenced to death by an English jury.

DURHAM   *(he releases JACQUES)* Look, my lad, how about going on a little trip till he cools down. Say Bermuda...

AUTH   Lord Durham—

DURHAM   *(to JACQUES)* Here's some pocket money... now split... fast.

AUTH   My hanging traitors is legal. Your exiling them isn't.

DURHAM   Bloodshed will only provoke more bloodshed. Generosity will snuff out the spark that could ignite a civil war.

AUTH   The best way to snuff out a civil war, m'lud, is to burn the house of every rebel in Lower Canada.

DURHAM   I cannot, I will not impose a military solution.[26]

AUTH	Then your presence in British North America is no longer required.

DURHAM exits.

ENGLISH	I burned the rebel's house, his barn, his crops, his church...
AUTH	And later, when, on Durham's recommendation, both Canadas became one...[27]
ENGLISH	I burned the Montreal parliament—
AUTH	Giving me the excuse to move the government to Ontario.
ENGLISH	Outside Quebec, the English language became a wave that virtually—

Sound. Traffic noises.

ENGLISH	That doesn't sound like a wave.

JACQUES and MARGOT enter singing. They mime cars beeping at each other.

PEGGY	What are you guys doing?

MARGOT sings "Life is a Highway." DAN enters as MACDONALD.

MAC	They're rolling down the Macdonald Cartier Highway—to Confederation!
JACQUES	Shouldn't Jacques Cartier be driving with him?
MAC	Not Jacques... the highway is named after George-Etienne Cartier. The francophone statesman who was almost as important as I was!

MARGOT   *(becoming GEORGE-ETIENNE CARTIER)* I
         was equally important!

MAC   My name is first on our highway.

GEORGE   We didn't build a highway. We built a rail-
         road.

MAC   You have to admit that was highway rob-
         bery.

JACQUES And all Canadians were railroaded.

         JACQUES exits.

MAC   But the railway "paved the road" to confed-
         eration.

GEORGE   You and I achieved an even-handed com-
         pact between our two peoples.

ENGLISH Two? Confederation created four equal
         provinces.

GEORGE   No, no, no. There was us on the one hand
         and you lot on the other.

PEGGY   *(breaking character)* Margot! My history
         book says that all provinces are equal!

MARGOT   My book says confederation promised an
         equal partnership between Quebec and the
         rest of you.

PEGGY   You mean... Francophones and
         Anglophones have different history books?
         (she turns to MACDONALD) Mr.
         Macdonald, what's the truth?

MAC   Ah... gotta go now. Choo, Choo. *(chugging
         away from them)*

PEGGY   *(following)* I need to know what you prom-
             ised Quebec.

MAC   Let me get back to you on that.

MARGOT   This could be really important in a century
             or so.

MAC   What's important to me is getting my choo
             choo to British Columbia. Choo Choo.
             (JACQUES throws himself in front of the train)
             Oops. Here's some silly body across the
             tracks.

JACQUES   I am the French speaking Métis nation. The
             prairie is my homeland and I demand—

MAC   Choo Choo. *(he runs over JACQUES)*
             Onward to the Rockies.

PEGGY   Wait a minute!

MARGOT   *(breaking character)* That was the Riel
             Rebellion you just ran over.

PEGGY   Shouldn't we act out the destruction of a
             whole nation?

MARGOT   They were the people Sam de Champlain
             dreamt of?

AUTH   It was the same story we acted out in
             Quebec. We provoked them again and
             again until they shot one of our guys. That
             gave us the excuse for wholesale slaughter.

MAC   I put the rebel leader on trial for treason.

MARGOT   Quebec begged mercy for the Métis.

MAC   I will hang Riel though every dog in
             Quebec howl.[28]

ALL   The resulting hatred lasts for generations.

AUTH   Manitoba becomes Anglophone. The
              Francophones must be assimilated.

PEGGY   Look, I'm getting really sick of hearing that.

MARGOT   *(to DAN)* Didn't you Anglophones ever
              consider an alternative to shooting people?

PEGGY   It's not Anglophones, Margot. It's men.
              (MARGOT shrugs) No, really, if women
              had had any power, our history would
              have been different.

**DAN &
JACQUES**   Hey now, girls...

PEGGY   Young women, pul-eeze.

JACQUES   We are still in THEN time, girls.

DAN   Yeah, girls, bras weren't invented. Let
              alone bra burners.

MARGOT   Peggy, when did women start to take
              action?

PEGGY   When they looked around the growing
              cities and saw...

              *They go to opposite sides of the stage. Sound.
              Virtual reality motif.*

**FRANCO
WOMAN**   *(seeing)* Children in Montreal working sixty
              hours a week for starvation wages...

**ANGLO
WOMAN**   Women in Toronto being paid half of what
              men earn...

BOTH   For the same work. Because all the bosses
              are men! *(they notice each other)*

DAN & **JACQUES**	Here it comes!
FRANCO **WOMAN**	*(to ANGLOPHONE WOMAN)* Excuse me...
JACQUES	The first wave of Feminism.
AUTH	Oh no!
ANGLO **WOMAN**	Can we talk?
DAN	No! You can't speak French.
JACQUES	You can't speak English!
BOTH	I speak a little. *(to each other)* Let's do lunch.
MARGOT	I know a Women's club in Montreal.

> *They change themselves into feminists.*
> *MARGOT's hat should have a veil, raised at*
> *the beginning of the scene. DAN can do any*
> *set up. Then he hangs out with AUTHOR-*
> *ITY and reacts with him.*

AUTH	Hey, Jacques. Take my... *(costume bit or prop)*
JACQUES	What for?
AUTH	I can't get into a Women's Club and I have to stop this alliance.
JACQUES	But I'm supposed to be a waiter in this scene.
AUTH	A waiter is a male, isn't he? A father, a husband?
JACQUES	Yeah...

AUTH   Then in 1900 you're qualified to represent authority.

DAN   *(assisting JACQUES with costume)* Right on.

**FRANCO
WOMAN**   *(to ANGLOPHONE WOMAN)* I want to share with you how Francophone feminists are improving education for the poor.

WAITER   May I recommend the Oeufs à l'estragon.

**FRANCO
WOMAN**   *(to the ANGLOPHONE WOMAN)* It's delicious.

WAITER   Perhaps Mrs. English would prefer a plain egg sandwich...

PEGGY   Well...

WAITER   On doughy rubber bread?

PEGGY   *(breaking character)* Hey, that's a stereotype.

MARGOT   Why?

PEGGY   He assumes I eat boring food just because I speak English. Besides, if the universal translator is working, you don't even know I'm Anglophone. *(the WAITER smiles while the FRANCOPHONE WOMAN hides a smile)* What are you two smirking at?

WAITER   Mrs. English did choose her own costume, I believe. *(MARGOT and the WAITER exchange another smile)*

**ANGLO
WOMAN**   *(rising)* I see no reason to sit here and be insulted.

AUTHORITY and DAN clap in glee.

MARGOT   Sit down. These women have more impor-
          tant things to talk about! *(to the WAITER)*
          Buzz off. *(to ANGLOPHONE WOMAN)*
          Now, we privileged women of Quebec are
          teaching underprivileged women to
          become better managers of money...

ANGLO
WOMAN   Good.

FRANCO
WOMAN   Also, we are trying to influence our own
          husbands to improve conditions for the
          poor and homeless.

ANGLO
WOMAN   Oh, oh! You won't need your husbands.
          We Anglophones have just accomplished
          something wonderful! *(she produces a ballot
          slip)*

FRANCO
WOMAN   What's this?

ANGLO
WOMAN   *(handing it to her)* The vote! Women have
          won the right to vote in the next election.

          *The FRANCOPHONE WOMAN reaches for
          it. The WAITER intercepts.*

WAITER   Madame, can you be thinking of touching
          such an unfeminine thing as politics?

FRANCO
WOMAN   Why... yes.

WAITER   Can you imagine what your church will say
          to this?

FRANCO
WOMAN   Oh.

WAITER	What your husband will say?
FRANCO WOMAN	My lover won't like it either.
WAITER	You won't have any man in your life if you become like her!
ANGLO WOMAN	How dare you?
WAITER	Who would love an ugly, squinting, *(ANGLOPHONE WOMAN hits him)* aggressive old maid—
FRANCO WOMAN	Stop!
WAITER	Who's going to force him to serve in the British army?
FRANCO WOMAN	*(silence)* I beg your pardon?
WAITER	Madame, while you are here chatting about bleeding heart Bolshevism, time has not stood still. It's 1917! The British and Germans are in the middle of World Bang Bang One.
FRANCO WOMAN	Is that true?
ANGLO WOMAN	It's the bang bang to end all bang bangs.
WAITER	They want to conscript your son, your husband, and your lover and turn them into cannon fodder.
ANGLO WOMAN	Quebec is part of the British Empire. French Canadians should fight for it!

WAITER	She's in favour of conscription! This vote for women is yet another Anglophone plot!
ANGLO WOMAN	But after the war, women can set about changing the world.
FRANCO WOMAN	*(lowering her veil)* Quebec is my world, Madame. Quebec, and my own family.
ANGLO WOMAN	No, please, don't—
WAITER	She has nothing more to say.
ANGLO WOMAN	She has the vote by federal law. You can't take it from her.
WAITER	She can choose not to exercise it. Or she can vote as I instruct her.
PEGGY	Oh, Margot please... can't you let us try to make things better?
MARGOT	You have to let her achieve equality in her own way, Peggy. *(to the WAITER)* And in her own time.

All exit. AUTHORITY is left alone on stage.

WAITER	I was able to keep the upper hand, and hold Quebec in the great darkness for the next fifty years. *(cupping an ear)* I don't hear a single wave. The dream of a French Nation must finally be forgotten.

Sound. Whispers become louder. "I remember. I remember." The others come on one by one. The following lines are distributed.

ALL   I remember. When I'm an Acadian in the sweat shops of Massachusetts, when I'm scrubbing floors at the Chateau Frontenac, when they passed illegal laws in Manitoba, New Brunswick and Saskatchewan to suppress the French language, when the Irish Catholics in Ontario banned French teaching from their schools, I remember. When I was drafted to fight British wars and it was speak English or be thrown in the brig, I remember.

Sound. Whispering. "Things must change. The hour of restoration is at hand. The hour of revolution is at hand."

AUTH   Revolution? If anyone was starting a revolution, I'd hear a tidal wave.

JACQUES   It's a revolution all right. But it's a quiet one.

MARGOT   It isn't an ocean wave...

Sound. "Things must change" repeated under the following, becoming insistent.

MARGOT   It is a river of tears that accumulated over centuries...

DAN   Give me a break!

MARGOT   ...but when the flood rises, *(MARGOT and PEGGY go to AUTHORITY and remove his costume)* it seems quite sudden.

JACQUES   When I couldn't even seek justice in French... je me souviens.

The actors all instantly revert to contemporary characters.

DAN   What?

MARGOT	What's wrong with the translator?
VOICE	The resolve in those words cannot be translated.
JACQUES	The nature of Canada has changed forever.
DAN	I guess the name of the game is no longer Monopoly.
PEGGY	With the advent of television... *(distributing sticks)* the name of the game...

Sound. The theme and sounds of "Hockey Night in Canada."

JACQUES	Come on Anglo—

JACQUES and DAN begin to play.

DAN	All right!
VOICE	I love hockey.
MARGOT	Then you're the referee.
JACQUES	Quebec becomes prosperous and modern. *(passing to MARGOT)*
MARGOT	*(breaking away)* We demand to be recognised as one of two founding nations.
DAN	*(saving)* The Prime Minster of the time stands for unhyphenated Canadianism.
PEGGY	The NDP adopts the Two Nations Policy at it's founding convention. 1961.
VOICE	She shoots. She scores!

Sound. Appropriate noises. JACQUES and MARGOT cheer.

PEGGY   Hold it.

                 Sound. A whistle.

PEGGY   That wasn't for *(pointing to JACQUES)*
                 their side.

DAN   Well, it sure wasn't for ours.

                 Sound. Hockey noises.

JACQUES   *(skating)* The Commission on Bilingualism
                 and Biculturalism. 1963.

VOICE   He scores. *(noises)* What a goal! And
                 Margot has the puck.

MARGOT   *(shooting)* Many Canadians welcome the
                 idea of Francophones as equal partners in
                 Canada.

DAN   *(saving)* Many Canadians object to having
                 French shoved down their throats.

MARGOT   It was not being shoved anywhere.

PEGGY   That's ridiculous, dad!

                 Sound. Whistle.

VOICE   Two minutes for high sticking.

                 DAN goes to the penalty box.

PEGGY   Canadians get their own flag! The Maple
                 Leaf.

JACQUES   So?

PEGGY   *(skating furiously)* So Canada isn't clinging
                 to the past.

MARGOT   *(intercepting)* Too little...

PEGGY   *(skating)* We're trying to show you that we can change!

MARGOT   *(intercepting)* Too late.

PEGGY   We're making room for francophones throughout the whole country.

JACQUES Quebec must become a country in its own right.

VOICE   Vivre le Québec libre!

JACQUES That was in the net!

DAN   *(from the box)* Off side! Off!

PEGGY   That's French interference in Canadian affairs.

VOICE   Wide of the goal posts. But here comes Margot...

MARGOT   Levesque launches the Parti Quebecois!

> *Scoring noises.*

DAN   *(back on)* 1969...

MARGOT   French...

PEGGY   And English...

MARGOT & PEGGY   Are both Official Languages in Canada.

MARGOT   That's my goal!

PEGGY   It's mine too!

MARGOT   You don't mean that.

PEGGY   Yes, I do. Honest.

Noises off.

VOICE   What's that? A fight in the stands!

JACQUES   The FLQ! The October crisis of '72! *(he cheers)*

MARGOT   Terrorism is not our goal. I don't want that score.

Sound. Amplified marching feet.

DAN   The government of Quebec requests Federal assistance. We send the Canadian army into Quebec!

VOICE   Two minutes for a knee-jerk reaction.

JACQUES   You jerk!

DAN and JACQUES engage in a brawl.

VOICE   Five minutes for fighting.

MARGOT   Computer, do something.

VOICE   But violence is the name of the game.

PEGGY   It doesn't have to be.

JACQUES   *(still brawling)* It's what people want!

DAN   Ask Don Cherry.

VOICE   Last minute of play in the second period.

MARGOT   The first referendum on Quebec Sovereignty.

Lots of noise.

VOICE   She shoots and... oh, misses.

*Sound. End of period noise. DAN and
JACQUES exit in opposite directions.*

MARGOT That was 1980... the year I was born...

PEGGY Me too.

MARGOT If we'd won the referendum, I would have
been born in my own country.

*MARGOT is depressed and turns away from
PEGGY.*

PEGGY I'm sorry you guys were disappointed. But
that was THEN. We're back in NOW time
now.

MARGOT So?

PEGGY So why are you still mad at ME?

MARGOT The problem with you Anglophones is you
always think it's about you. It isn't. It's
about me being able to just be me.

PEGGY Okay, I'll try to understand that. I'll try not
to stand in your road.

MARGOT Yeah? Then maybe we can be friends. But
what about your dad?

PEGGY What about YOUR dad!

MARGOT He's a nice man... except about
Anglophones.

PEGGY So is mine... except he has
Francophonephobia.

MARGOT I guess a lot of their generation is kinda
trapped into bigotry.

PEGGY So... what do you think we should do?

MARGOT I guess we have to—like—think for our-selves?

       Hockey noises as the next half begins. DAN and JACQUES reappear.

PEGGY So are you thinking—

MARGOT —what I'm thinking?

       They look at each other and nod.

PEGGY Dad,

MARGOT Dad, the way you and he play the game is kinda... well... outdated.

MARGOT & PEGGY We don't want to be Anglophone against Francophone anymore, so—

MARGOT Peggy and I are starting our own team.

PEGGY It's going to be the Communication team versus the Non-Communication team.

JACQUES Did she say Non?

MARGOT Yes.

JACQUES This hockey game is a federalist plot!

DAN *(at the same time)* This hockey game is a Separatist plot.

MARGOT That's so typical! Okay, we're going to call you the Knee-Jerk team.

PEGGY Our team is going to be called "A little intelligence."

MARGOT   Or "respect for each other."

**JACQUES
& DAN**   Pul-eeze! There's no way I'm playing with him.

MARGOT   Fine! Don't play.

PEGGY   We can score all the goals we want.

MARGOT   1982. The charter of Rights and Freedoms.

PEGGY   Canada's own constitution.

JACQUES   *(jumping into the game)* Quebec says no!

DAN   The rest of Canada goes ahead.

MARGOT   I knew they couldn't sit on the sidelines.

JACQUES   You can't redefine Confederation without us!

They brawl. Whistle.

VOICE   The entire knee-jerk team gets five minutes for fighting among themselves.

DAN and JACQUES go off.

**MARGOT
& PEGGY**   Time for a major Power Play.

Without opposition MARGOT and PEGGY score a goal to wild cheering.

PEGGY   The Ontario legislature guarantees some government services in French. 1986.

VOICE   Margot passes to Peggy...

MARGOT   The Meech Lake Accord. 1987.

VOICE	Peggy shoots... and—
MARGOT	Did it go in?
VOICE	Misses!
MARGOT	Oh, Peggy.
JACQUES	I told you, there's no point trying to play with an Anglophone.
PEGGY	A lot of us did our best, eh?
JACQUES	We Quebecers despair of ever getting agreement.

DAN enters as the NATIVE.

NATIVE	Exactly whom do you mean by we, white-man?

The game stops.

ALL	What!
NATIVE	You'd forgotten about me, hadn't you?
PEGGY	I guess we did.
NATIVE	Well, the aboriginal has regained his voice in NOW time, and *(to JACQUES)* you cannot speak for Quebec and Canada without including me. There's a lot of other cultures you don't speak for either.
MARGOT	He's absolutely right, Dad.
VOICE	He is wrong. Assimilation is inevitable.
MARGOT & PEGGY	No, it isn't!

VOICE   There can only be one kind of people in a
nation.

**MARGOT
& PEGGY**   No!

VOICE   Because that's what a nation is. One must
be superior—

**MARGOT
& PEGGY**   No!

VOICE   —and all others inferior.

ALL   No, no, no, no, NO!

JACQUES   Even I don't think like that any more.

NATIVE   A country can exist by creating bonds
between peoples...

MARGOT   Such as love of freedom... *(DAN and
JACQUES exit)*

PEGGY   A country can be held together by respect
for law and human rights.

NATIVE   And by the dreams we share for our children's future.

**PEGGY &
MARGOT**   Right on.

VOICE   Then why on earth did you two start a war
game?

PEGGY   Who's playing a War Game?

    *Sound. Reprise of opening Space War
    sequence.*

VOICE   Remember?

MARGOT   Okay, we were.

PEGGY   But we tried to turn you off.

VOICE   Hate is easy to turn on. It's hard to turn off.

PEGGY &
MARGOT   Who said anything about hate?

VOICE   You turned me on because you hate English!

MARGOT   Oh... just sometimes.

VOICE   And you hate French.

PEGGY &
MARGOT   Actually, it's homework I really hate.

PEGGY   I mean, I know learning French is—like a good idea.

MARGOT   I guess it's okay to have a second language. Okay, maybe it's better than okay.

VOICE   You had great hate after the Conquest, and after the rebellion!

MARGOT   Only because you had us trapped in the Past.

VOICE   I still have you trapped in my hard drive. I want more bang, bang!

MARGOT   Is that why your keeping us here?

VOICE   Pick a card. Come on... pick a card.

PEGGY   He's hoping for another war or something!

VOICE   (singing) We fired our guns and the British kept a'coming—

MARGOT   Hey, computer...

VOICE   *(singing)* We fired again and—

PEGGY   Forget it!

MARGOT   I will never, ever—

PEGGY   —no matter what,

**PEGGY &
MARGOT**   Shoot anybody!

VOICE   Then playing won't be any fun.

The computer spits out JACQUES and DAN.

DAN   Are we free?

JACQUES   On est libre?

VOICE   The universal translator is deactivated.

MARGOT   Essayons de trouver une sortie.

DAN   What did she say?

PEGGY   Toi, pas la.

DAN   What!

MARGOT   *(in English)* We're still walled in.

JACQUES   Qu'est ce qu'elle dit?

MARGOT   *(in French)* Elle et moi, on se comprend, P'pa—

PEGGY   —meme sans traducteur. Like we're cousins, eh?

DAN   Who cares!

MARGOT   We want to talk to each other.

JACQUES   Pourquoi?

DAN   (*miming walls frantically*) Talk won't get us out of here!

MARGOT   Mais, oui—

DAN   We're still trapped.

> *JACQUES is also miming walls and runs into DAN. They jostle.*

MARGOT   P'pa—

DAN   Out of my way!

PEGGY   Dad! The computer gets turned on by conflict.

MARGOT   You just stay still, okay?

PEGGY   And be polite to each other. (*the dads open their mouths*) Puleeze.

MARGOT & PEGGY   Together—

MARGOT   On va se sortir de cette boite-ci.

PEGGY   We'll get us out of the box we're in.

VOICE   I can't stand this mush! Game over.

> *They find an opening.*

PEGGY   Way to go!

MARGOT   Way!

> *The dads approach the opening at the same time and bump into each other. Then both stand back and bow the other through. They become caught in "After you", "Non, after you" mime. The girls reach back and drag them through.*

PEGGY   *(French pronunciation)* Super!

MARGOT   C'est full cool!

The End

Footnotes

1. Iroquoian translation of Canada; Jacques Cartier; Voltaire; UN Report; Bouchard.
2. On his first voyage in 1534. Cartier kidnapped the two sons of Donnacona. He took them to France but returned them the next year.
3. Cabot lands at Bonavista, Newfoundland, 1497.
4. See "When Two Worlds Meet," in *The Illustrated History of Canada*, ed. Craig Brown.
5. On the Bay of Fundy, and in Conception Bay, Newfoundland.
6. See "Colonization and Conflict," in *The Illustrated History of Canada*, ed. Craig Brown.
7. ibid., 1609 Champlain shot three Iroquois chiefs to cement his alliance with the Hurons.
8. Abraham Martin, for whom the Plains are named, has descendants who beacame Protestant Anglophones post Conquest.
9. Huron is derived from a French word indicating bushman.
10. Between 1663 and 1673, 775 French orphan girls were sent to New France by Louis 14. Each was given a dowry worth about half a year's average wage.
11. Craig Brown, *The Illustrated History of Canada* page 138-43 doesn't mention women in the illicit trade, nor does Newman, but women historians do.
12. See Craig Brown, *The Illustrated History of Canada* page 166.
13. When Radisson's proposal to re-organize the fur trade was rebuffed by French authorities, he and his brother-in-law turned to England. The Company of Adventurers (Hudson'd Bay) received a Royal Charter from Charles the second in 1670.
14. 1749
15. 1756-63 in Europe.
16. 7,000 Acadians were deported by the British in 1755.
17. Fall of Quebec, 1759
18. 1760
19. Treaty of Paris, 1763.
20. McNaught The Pelican History of Canada.
21. Papineau, May 1837.
22. The uniform of the Upper Canadian rebels of 1837 had two white stars – the sister stars of liberty representing Lower and Upper Canada. Mckenzie and Papineau had correspondence testifying to their hope to unite their causes. Brown, *The Wait Letters*.

[23] There is a Canadian painting of the period which shows the Governor kicking a woman as she kneels before him. It's titled "Sir George Arthur Spurns Mrs. Lount With His Foot." Samuel Lount was hanged for treason after the Toronto rebellion.

[24] Schull, *Rebellion*.

[25] December 13, 1837.

[26] After the British Parliament refused to ratify Durham's decision to exile rebels to Bermuda (not a penal colony), he resigned saying "The only solution is a military one which I could not implement as well as a soldier. And I would not even if I could".

[27] Act of Union 1840 and Montreal riots over Rebellion Losses act 1849.

[28] John A. Macdonald.

Sources

Brown, Craig, ed. *The Illustrated History of Canada.* Lester Publishing, 1996.

McNaught, Kenneth. *The Pelican History of Canada.* Penguin, 1969.

Wade, Mason. *The French Canadians.* Macmillan, 1968.

MacKirdy, K.A., J.S. Moir, and Y.F. Zoltvany. *Changing Perspectives in Canadian History.* Dent and Sons Canada Ltd., 1971.

Brown, Robert Craig, and Ramsay Cook. Canada, A Nation Transformed. McClelland and Stewart.

Lucas, C.P., ed. *Lord Durham's Report on the Affairs of British North America.*

Trofminkoff, Susan Mann. *The Dream of a Nation.* Gage, 1983.

Schull, Joseph. *Rebellion.* Macmillan, 1971.

Reid, J.H.S., K. McNaught, and H.S. Crowe. *A Source-Book of Canadian History.* Toronto, 1964.

OTHER TITLES BY ANNE CHISLETT

ANOTHER SEASON'S PROMISE
Written with Keith Roulston.
2 acts   6m/4f/1 child
DPS (pb)   # 807 $ 6.00

THE GIFT
1 act   1m/4 teens
PUC (cs)   1-55155-204-3 $ 7.00

GLENGARRY SCHOOL DAYS
Written with Janet Amos.
2 acts   7m/2f (10 or more children)
PUC (cs)   1-55173-149-5 $ 9.00

QUIET IN THE LAND
2 acts   6m/4f/2 or 4 children
PUC (cb)   1-55173-292-0 (1997) $ 11.00

THE TOMORROW BOX
2 acts   2m/3f
PLCN (tpb)   0-88754-198-4 (1986) $ 10.95

VENUS SUCKED IN: A POST-FEMINIST COMEDY
In the collection *Airborne*. Radio Play.
16 scenes   4f
BLI (pb)   0-921368-22-4 (1991) $ 14.95

YANKEE NOTIONS
2 acts   7m/4f
PLCN (tpb)   0-88754-497-5 (1993) $ 10.95

Available from Playwrights Union of Canada
416-703-0201   fax 703-0059
orders@puc.ca   http://www.puc.ca